ALEXANDER DONIPHAN

COURAGEOUS DEFENDER & FRIEND
OF THE SAINTS

SUSAN EASTON BLACK

Covenant Communications, Inc.

Cover design by Hannah Bischoff

Cover design copyright © 2022 by Covenant Communications, Inc.

Published by Covenant Communications, Inc.
American Fork, Utah

Printed in the United States of America
First Printing: April 2022

29 28 27 26 25 24 23 22   10 9 8 7 6 5 4 3 2 1

ISBN: 978-1-52442-197-7

ALEXANDER DONIPHAN

COURAGEOUS DEFENDER & FRIEND OF THE SAINTS

OTHER BOOKS AND AUDIOBOOKS
BY SUSAN EASTON BLACK

400 Questions and Answers about the Book of Mormon

400 Questions and Answers about the Old Testament

*400 Questions and Answers about the
Life and Times of Jesus Christ*

400 Questions and Answers about the Doctrine and Covenants

Women of Character

Men of Character

Glorious Truths about Mother Eve

Glorious Truths about Mary, Mother of Jesus

Glorious Truths about Emma Smith

Glorious Truths about Women of the Restoration

The Other Martyr: Insights from the Life of Hyrum Smith

To my grandson
Reef
courage is a choice

TABLE OF CONTENTS

INTRODUCTION

ON NOVEMBER 1, 1839, ALEXANDER Doniphan was ordered to carry out the execution of Joseph Smith and his fellow prisoners:

> Sir:—You will take Joseph Smith and the other prisoners into the public square of Far West, and shoot them at 9 o'clock to-morrow morning.
>
>   Samuel D. Lucas
>   Major-General Commanding[1]

Rather than comply with his superior officer's order, Doniphan took the moral high ground and responded to Major General Lucas:

> It is cold-blooded murder. I will not obey your order. My brigade shall march for Liberty tomorrow morning, at 8 o'clock; and if you execute these men, I will hold you responsible before an earthly tribunal, so help me God!
>
>   A.W. Doniphan
>   Brigadier-General[2]

---

1   Joseph Smith, *History of the Church of Jesus Christ of Latter-day Saints* (Salt Lake City: The Church of Jesus Christ of Latter-day Saints, 1905), 3:246.
2   Smith, *History of the Church*, 3:246.

I grew up thinking few men were as courageous as Alexander Doniphan. He risked his reputation and standing in the military in favor of a moral right. To me, he was a hero—a man who could not be swayed.

Since then, I have learned that Alexander Doniphan was a complex man who had innumerable admirers but few close friends. He had opinions that were rarely popular with the majority, but their disapproval didn't bother him. His belief in the Manifest Destiny of the United States led him to enlist as a private in the Mexican-American War. By the time the war ended, he held the rank of colonel. Though he favored the Deep South in heritage and culture, Alexander Doniphan spoke of keeping the nation together rather than splitting the nation along the Mason-Dixon Line. When asked to run for governor of Missouri, he declined, choosing his family over politics.

At the Washington Peace Conference of 1861, President Abraham Lincoln said to Doniphan, "And this is the Colonel Doniphan who made the wonderful march from Santa Fé to Monterey against both the Indians and Mexicans. Now, colonel, permit me to say you are the only man connected with any great military enterprise who ever came up . . . to my expectations."[3] Far from feeling complimented by President Lincoln's words, Doniphan wrote his true feelings in a letter to his nephew John Doniphan on February 22, 1862: "It is very humiliating for an American to know that the present and future destiny of his country is wholly in the hands of one man and that such a man is Lincoln."[4]

Alexander Doniphan was not in step with his colleagues, his friends, or President Lincoln. Doniphan was his own man. He had strong opinions that were not subject to change. Despite his

---

3   D. C. Allen, *A Sketch of the Life and Character of Col. Alexander W. Doniphan* (Liberty, MO, 1897), 27–28, in Joseph Dawson, *Doniphan's Epic March: The First Missouri Volunteers in the Mexican War* (Lawrence, KS: University Press of Kansas, 1999), 1.

4   Letter from Alexander Doniphan to John Doniphan, February 22, 1861, quoted in Gregory Maynard, "Alexander William Doniphan, The Forgotten Man from Missouri," (master's thesis, Brigham Young University, 1973), 95.

unwavering and stubborn personality, the people who knew him best admired him most. Doniphan was a brave man whose nobleness of soul and fierce loyalty to moral correctness made him one of the greatest Americans of the nineteenth century.

There is much to learn about the life of Alexander Doniphan. The purpose of *Alexander Doniphan: Courageous Defender & Friend of the Saints* is not to present a complete biography of his life. Remarkable biographies have already been written by Roger D. Launius—*Alexander William Doniphan: Portrait of a Missouri Moderate* (1997)—and Joseph G. Dawson—*Doniphan's Epic March: The 1st Missouri Volunteers in the Mexican War* (1999). The purpose of this work is to present glimpses into the life of a courageous man whose moral compass was set. This work would not have been possible without the capable assistance of McKenna Swindle and Eliza Allen.

CHAPTER ONE
Childhood and Youth

ON JULY 9, 1808, WHEN Thomas Jefferson was president of the United States, and Mason County, Kentucky, was part of the Deep South, Alexander William Doniphan was born. Known as Will to his friends, he was the youngest in his family of ten, living along the banks of the Ohio River near Maysville, Kentucky. He was named for his grandfathers, Alexander Doniphan and William Smith, proud military men of Virginia. His paternal grandfather had guarded the frontiers in the upper region of Richmond, Virginia, so that settlers scattered along the rivers could rest assured that their plantations were safe from American Indian attacks. His maternal grandfather, Captain William Smith, had protected his countrymen as well as their property as a soldier in the Virginia light horse militia.

His Parents

Doniphan's parents, Joseph Doniphan and Anne Fowke Smith, were products of their Southern upbringing. Joseph Doniphan, like his father before him, had served in the military. Joseph enlisted in the Revolutionary War to fight against the tyranny of Great Britain. He fought in the battles at Yorktown and was present when General Cornwallis surrendered on October 19, 1781, and a free America was born.

With the war behind him and youthful adventures ahead, Joseph joined Daniel Boone and headed west. Doniphan wrote, "My father came to Kentucky with Daniel Boone, just at the close of the Revolution. [He] taught the first school ever taught in Kentucky—at the solicitation of the families at Boonsborough."[1] During that year, when not teaching school, fighting American Indians, hunting, or felling trees, twenty-two-year-old Joseph Doniphan returned to Virginia to court his sweetheart, Anne Smith.

Joseph and Anne were wed April 25, 1784, in Fairfax County, Virginia, near George Washington's Mount Vernon home along the Potomac River. After six years of marriage and the birth of three children, Joseph was still regaling his wife, Anne, with stories of his year in Kentucky with Daniel Boone. When he learned of neighbors moving to the expansive green pastures of Kentucky, there was little that could keep Joseph in Virginia.

The Doniphans in Mason County, Kentucky

In 1790, Joseph and Anne Doniphan and their children left their moorings in Virginia and headed to Kentucky. They put down stakes and settled along the Ohio River in Kenton's Station, five miles west of Maysville—the county seat of Mason County. It was the same area where, earlier, Daniel Boone had set up a trading post and built a tavern. It was the very place Joseph had dreamed of living in for years.

The Doniphans' move was not as we might imagine—a young family having little and eking out a living, scratching the ground and felling trees like most pioneers coming to Kentucky. Joseph Doniphan was not an upper-tier Southerner who had left a mansion and row houses of slaves behind in Virginia,

---

1 *Journal of William H. Richardson, a Private Soldier in the Campaign of New and Old Mexico under the Command of Colonel Doniphan of Missouri*, 3rd ed. (New York: William H. Richardson, 1848), 195; William McGroarty, "William H. Richardson's Journal of Doniphan's Expedition," *Missouri Historical Review* 22, no. 2 (January 1928): 202.

but he was not a pauper either. Joseph had slaves to work his fields and money to fulfill his dreams. It did not take long before he became a prosperous gentleman farmer in Kenton's Station. From crops to investments in the region, nothing of a financial nature soured in his hands. He shipped hemp and tobacco to market on barges from the Maysville port along the Ohio River. With his ever-increasing prosperity came a greater sense of dignity to him—a sense of entitlement.

To keep undesirables from trespassing on his land or stealing his slaves, Joseph used his military skills, which served himself and his community. He was elected by townsfolk to be the sheriff of Maysville. Few ne'er-do-wells wanted to tangle with Sherriff Joseph Doniphan. He was not only a formidable officer of the law; he was also an up-and-coming gentleman who embraced the Southern ways. He had wealth, toiling slaves, a good marriage, and a military presence about him.

Doniphan's Father Dies

"My father died in March, 1813, when I was less than five years old," Doniphan said.[2] Joseph's death at Clark's Run in Mason County was unexpected, yet days before his demise, Joseph wrote his last will and testament. In that legal document, he named as beneficiaries his wife and their seven living children: Thomas Smith Doniphan (age twenty-six), George Doniphan (age twenty-three), Margaret Doniphan (age twenty-one), Susannah Doniphan (age nineteen), Lucy Doniphan (age nine), Matilda Doniphan (age nine), and Alexander William Doniphan (age four).

With her older children starting families of their own, Joseph's widow, Anne, had only her twin daughters and Alexander to rear. She had the necessary means to care for these children. According to the civil records of 1813, she owned an estate in the Ohio River town of Augusta, tracts of land in Maysville, and eighteen slaves.

---

2   McGroarty, *Missouri Historical Review*, 202.

As for four-year-old Doniphan, his father wanted more for his last son than fleeting memories. He bequeathed to him a slave named Stephen and a generous portion of farmland. At first glance, it appears his last-born son was poised to succeed in life. Such was not the case. Land in Kentucky was nearly free for the taking in 1813, and one slave could not do the work of many. Nineteenth-century Kentuckians viewed education— not land and one slave—as the gateway to opportunity. Land left to a mere lad, not yet of school age, in a backwoods community, would hamper the boy's chance of scholastic attainment and his chance at ever becoming a true Southern gentleman.

Enrolls in the Augusta College

Facing the challenge of having three young children at home and the task of running an estate as well as managing eighteen slaves was quite a burden for Anne Smith Doniphan, but she was up to the task. Doniphan explained, "My mother was a bright woman and for some years trained me well—but there being no school, and even the poor one a mile and half away, I was sent to Augusta, KY."[3]

In Augusta, nineteen miles northwest of Maysville, Doniphan lived with his brother George (who was eighteen years Doniphan's senior) and George's wife, Mary Ann Marshall Doniphan.

At age fourteen, Doniphan enrolled in the Augusta Methodist Episcopal Academy. The academy, often referred to as a college, was chartered on December 7, 1822, by the Kentucky legislature. The academy boasted that their professors' ability to educate the young was unrivaled. "We had seven preachers filling the professors' chairs, and to them, under Providence, I owe all that I have been and am," Doniphan wrote. "My morals became fixed, my habits of industry established, and love of literature absorbing."[4]

3   William B. McGroarty, "William H. Richardson's Journal of Doniphan's Expedition," *Missouri Historical Review* 22, no. 2 (January 1928): 202.
4   McGroarty, *Missouri Historical Review*, 202.

Dr. Henry B. Bascom, "a minister famed for his eloquence in the pulpit, taught Doniphan . . . the power of rhetoric to sway audiences and the complexity of reasoning necessary to every jeremiad." Richard Keene, "a learned but eccentric Irishman," insisted that Doniphan study "the ideas and philosophies of the Enlightenment—engendering a commitment to republican ideals, a belief in reason and moderation, and a respect for the rights of others." Keene was devoted to rational thinking yet had a strong appreciation for the creative eloquence of poetry. He pushed Doniphan to study the "works of the great poets because of their use of language to move people." Keene said, "Through knowledge of the poets could alone come the precise meaning of words, the perfect pronunciation of them, the melody of speech, and the majestic declamation of the orator."[5]

At age eighteen, Doniphan graduated with honors from the Augusta Academy. With graduation behind him and new vistas awaiting, it could be assumed that he would return to his inheritance and become a gentlemen farmer like his father. After all, he could quote literature at will and was, in many respects, on his way to becoming a Southern gentleman.

But for Doniphan, that's not what he wanted. He didn't want to be locked into farmland and to mingle with the same neighbors he had always known. As he tried to figure out his destiny, he stayed in his brother's home and studied ancient and modern English literature on his own. Clever phrases and the twists and turns of plots were much to his liking but did not lead to a career path other than a gentleman who could converse about the classics.

The Honorable Martin Pickett Marshall

How Doniphan determined that the law would suit his fancy had much to do with the Honorable Martin P. Marshall. Marshall was not only a renowned attorney in Augusta, he

5 A. W. Doniphan to D. C. Allen, February 4, 1874, quoted in Roger D. Launius, *Alexander William Doniphan: Portrait of a Missouri Moderate* (Columbia, MO: University of Missouri Press, 1997), 3.

was the father of Mary Ann Doniphan—the wife of George Doniphan—and cousin to the venerable chief justice of the Supreme Court, John Marshall.

Martin Marshall had watched young Doniphan mature to manhood in George and Mary Ann's home and was aware of his scholastic achievements at the Augusta Academy. At age fifty, Martin Marshall saw in young Doniphan a prodigy—a rising star. Doniphan saw in Marshall an opportunity to learn from the best and began his studies in the Marshall Law Office.

Martin Marshall encouraged his young protégé to appreciate the evolving legal system and the rule of law. Of his mentor, Doniphan said, "His legal preceptor was one of the most learned and able of all the members of the famous Marshall family."[6] D. C. Allen remarked,

> [Marshall] required his pupil to read and carefully study portions of the classical authors of the English language. . . . It was, as Mr. Marshall phrased it, to fructify and chasten the pupil's imagination and give him wings for more arduous flights. Secondly, he required him to read the histories of England and America and cognate works, so that he might see, historically, the evolution of our system of law. And, thirdly, he required of him a most careful study of those text-books of the law which were then considered necessary in order to [gain] admission to practice.[7]

With such a mentor, it is not surprising that Doniphan successfully passed the bar in Kentucky in 1829. Since Cincinnati was only sixty miles from Augusta, he crossed the Ohio River and

6   William Elsey Connelley, *Doniphan's Expedition and the Conquest of New Mexico and California* (Kansas City, MO: Bryant and Douglas Book and Stationary Company, 1907), 21.

7   Hughes, Allen, and Morehead, *Doniphan's Expedition and The Conquest of New Mexico and California*, 21.

successfully petitioned the Ohio Supreme Court for admission to the state bar. At this point, two states had welcomed Doniphan as an attorney. He was not yet twenty-one years old.

Doniphan Returns to His Moorings

Decades after leaving his childhood home, Doniphan returned to his moorings. He hired a driver and a carriage to take him and a friend to "many old familiar spots and especially the schoolboy spots." In Maysville, he searched for the graves of his parents "on the farm on which I was born. . . . I had no knowledge of the condition in which the graves were, as . . . I had not been there since I was quite a lad, and of course the country and especially the roads and passways had wholly changed." Unfortunately, the "carriage was overturned on a steep hillside by the awkwardness of the driver; falling on the lower side, my friend's whole weight came on me, the concussion was so severe that for an hour I thought the chances of life and death were greatly against me." But typical of Doniphan, "I started on; found the graves of my loved and revered parents in excellent repair, having in my brother's lifetime been walled in with a heavy stone fence." He then went to the "house in which I was born. [I ate] pears off the trees my father had planted from Virginia seed 90 years ago."[8]

---

8 William B. McGroarty, "Letters from Alexander W. Doniphan," *Missouri Historical Review* 24, no. 1 (October 1929): 38.

CHAPTER TWO
A Lawyer in Lexington, Missouri

IN HIS EARLY TWENTIES, DONIPHAN was a striking figure. He stood six feet four inches in height, had thick auburn hair, and was clean-shaven. Contemporary D. C. Allen described him as "well proportioned, altogether dignified in appearance, and gentle in his manners . . . his bright hazel eye[s] discerning, keen and expressive."[1] Biographer Roger D. Launius described him as having an "impressive bearing, powerful physique, handsome features, and dynamic character [which] made him especially attractive to women."[2] From Doniphan's outward appearance, it looked like the world was his for the taking.

With inherited farmland awaiting his supervision and doting family members pleading for him to stay, the logical choice for Doniphan was to put down stakes and carve out a living in Kentucky. But the lure of Missouri beckoned. Doniphan packed his belongings and headed west in search of greener pastures, much like his father before him. With law credentials in hand and the enthusiasm of a reckless youth, Doniphan moved to the Missouri frontier unfettered by family or friends.

---

1   Roger D. Launius, *Alexander William Doniphan: Portrait of a Missouri Moderate* (Columbia, MO: University of Missouri, 1997), 3.
2   Launius, *Alexander William Doniphan*, 5.

He never saw his family or his mentor Martin Marshall again. This suited him, for he wanted his destiny to be of his own making.

Lexington, Missouri

In 1830, twenty-one-year-old Doniphan linked his future with Missouri, a slave state admitted to the Union only nine years before. He was given an audience before the Missouri Supreme Court on April 19, 1830. Standing in front of the formidable judges, he asked for a license to practice law in their state. He was granted the license based on his earlier admissions to the bar in Kentucky and Ohio.

More confident than ever, Doniphan settled in Lexington, the seat of Lafayette County. Lexington was the largest city west of St. Louis. The rich bottomlands that ran along the Missouri River were ideal for plantation-style agriculture and had attracted Southerners with deep pockets and big plans. Being situated in the central-western part of the state, Lexington had a reputation as the commercial center, a transshipment port for merchandise, which was stockpiled on docks before moving on to Independence and the overland Santa Fe Trail.

Full of youthful confidence, Doniphan opened a law office on the courthouse square in the downtown center of Lexington. In so doing, he joined a near tsunami-like wave of two thousand newcomers to Lexington, most tracing their roots to the Deep South—Virginia, Kentucky, Tennessee, and the Carolinas. They were a hardy stock, like Doniphan, born of soldiers who were not afraid to die or take risks. Many had blazed trails, subdued the wilderness, and faced off wild animals and, in their eyes, even wilder American Indians. The newcomers had brought with them hundreds of slaves, extending the Southern lifestyle to what some were calling the most western outpost of the United States.

A few of the Southerners had staked out claims to large sweeping plantations using their slaves to plant and harvest commercial crops, such as hemp and tobacco. The more modest

Southerner raised a variety of vegetables, fruits, and livestock for sale locally, nothing more. Whether large landowners or "two-bit" farmers, the Southerners in Lexington were Doniphan's kind of people. He understood and accepted their culture, having grown up in Kentucky. He didn't question the moral or legal implication of such traditions as slavery; it was just how it was and had been for generations of his kin.

A Lawyer in the Fifth Judicial Circuit

Living among the residents of Lexington for nearly three years, Doniphan gained notoriety as an attorney in the Missouri Fifth Judicial Circuit. The circuit covered more than twenty-five hundred square miles and extended on both sides of the Missouri River to the western boundary of the state. This meant Doniphan was on horseback much of the time. He spent several days each month riding the circuit from town to town, searching for a court. Since few courthouses dotted the Missouri landscape, court cases were seldom heard in a courthouse. Doniphan's cases were more often heard before judge and jury in taverns and small log cabins that had been commandeered for the occasion.

Doniphan recalled "regularly attend[ing] the courts in ten counties. The formation of new counties often changed the courts, (but not their number,) in which I practiced."[3] In recalling his days of riding in the Fifth Judicial Circuit, he said,

> Nearing the close of a weary day's travel on horse-
> back, nothing was more cheering than the sight
> of the curling smoke of a cabin, with no fear of
> refusal—even to a stranger. Alighting, most prob-
> ably the sturdy host was preparing his gun, ram-
> rod and ammunition for the morrow's hunt. The
> bright, cheery housewife, in home-spun dress,

---

3   Alexander William Doniphan, *Address by Col. Alexander Doniphan*, Delivered Liberty, MO., June 5, 1872 on the Occasion of the Celebration of the People of Clay County, of the 50th Anniversary of the County's Establishment, 5–6, quoted in Launius, *Alexander William Doniphan*, 8.

often of the inevitable Tennessee stripe, would be
busily engaged in preparing the evening meal for
the returned hunter. Often have I met with the
accident of a dinner as the juicy venison ribs were
roasting before a bright, wood fire in the ample
fire place. . . . If the host was from Tennessee—as
was often the case—he would easily glide into a
social chat by asking about General Jackson. . . .
We were not then a nation of readers; few jour-
nals reached the country;—hence the inquiries.
It would have been unkind not to have gratified
their patriotic anxiety, and I never failed to do so,
either from my own limited store of reliable information, or more frequently, from the ample stores
of youthful imagination. The rule was: horse well
cared for, comfortable night, smoking breakfast,
and nothing ever to pay. Indeed, the most deli-
cate diplomacy was required in making the offer so as to avoid giving offense to your generous
entertainer. For twenty years after my arrival [in
Missouri], I do not remember paying a bill at a
farm house.[4]

At first, Doniphan took any client, even ones assigned to
him by the judge of the Fifth Judicial Circuit. But as Doniphan's
reputation increased, so did the demand on his time.

His ability to draw a crowd and convince a jury of the innocence
of his clients had much to do with his being a masterful speaker
in an era that valued oratory. His courtroom antics resembled a
debater more than the library persona of a prestigious legal scholar.
His plausible approach to any argument, interspersed with a flair
for theatrics and expletives, assured him a crowded courtroom.

Once, an alleged criminal defended by another attorney paid
extra for Doniphan to give the summation remarks before the

---

4   Doniphan, *Address*, 5, quoted in Launius, *Alexander William Doniphan*, 6–7.

jury adjourned to decide the defendant's fate. When Doniphan gave the closing argument on behalf of this client—and others—juries, judges, and spectators alike were moved to tears.

Doniphan was a master in the courtroom. He had control at all times. When the courtroom heated up in angry debate, Doniphan would stand, speak in a high-pitched tone, and pull on his sleeves in a nervous tug. The district court judge, wanting order in his courtroom, would gavel the courtroom to order and demand that Doniphan modulate his voice and take his seat. Ignoring the heavy sound of the gavel and demands of the judge, Doniphan would pull his sleeves ever higher and raise his voice louder to a shrill.

His courtroom performances were so legendary that one judge issued a verdict of "not guilty," forgetting to ask the decision of the gentlemen of the jury. On that occasion, Doniphan, not the freed defendant, was carried on the shoulders of spectators out of the courtroom to great applause. It is no wonder that Doniphan's contemporaries characterized him as an absolute master at the bar and claimed that the swarming blackbirds overhead grew silent in admiration of his craft.

One rustic frontiersman, who knew little of Southern graces and too much of the woods, said of Doniphan's court appearances,

> It came around to Doniphan, and instantly there was a great rush of people from all around to the speakers' stand. At the very first, I paid no particular attention to it. As he went on, he charmed not only the people, but the birds and the wild animals. I discovered that the trees around the speakers' stand were all full of birds and squirrels, chattering and barking away. He even charmed the birds and the squirrels out of their lairs. I never saw such an affect produced on people as he made that day. He was young,

very tall and splendid looking with a voice very
keen, which rang through the woods, an eye that
flashed lightning.[5]

Doniphan could explain a law so simply that even the
uneducated knew he spoke the truth. He reasoned his arguments
step-by-step with such precision that not even a knife could cut
through his case with more accuracy. But what revealed his genius
more than any other trait was the fact that he never prepared
his courtroom speeches. He delivered them extemporaneously
with no notes and little forethought. His delivery and message
often won him praise from even his most ardent opponents. His
language was beautiful, his gestures graceful, and his striking
presence unmatched. D. C. Allen said, "What an orator he was!
Men who had been in Congress used to say that Webster and
Clay could not sway men as could old Alex Doniphan. He may
have been bashful before he began, but once under way he was
on fire."[6]

As his legal reputation spread, Doniphan was asked to
assist attorney Abiel Leonard in a murder trial. Doniphan
hesitated, believing such a trial was beyond his training. It was
only after Leonard assured Doniphan that he was qualified that
he agreed. His presentation at the murder trial was unrehearsed
and genuine, and his "conduct in this trial was modest, and gave
evidence of the dawning of the reputation as a criminal lawyer
which he afterward attained." Years later, Doniphan wrote that
he made his "first speech in defence of a criminal charged with
murder he had ever heard, never having witnessed a trial for
murder before."[7]

5   Floyd Calvin Shoemaker, "Alexander W. Doniphan, 1808–1887 Solider; Lawyer;
and Orator," *Missouri's Hall of Fame: Lives of Eminent Missourians*, quoted in Alexander
Doniphan Committee, *The Will of Missouri: The Life, Times & Influence of Alexander William
Doniphan* (Kansas City, MO: Woodneath Press, 2020), 19.
6   Alexander Doniphan Committee, *The Will of Missouri*, 18.
7   Doniphan to Allen, "Sketch of Life," 4, quoted in Launius, *Alexander William Doniphan*,
8.

Doniphan would go on to defend dozens of men accused of murder, which says as much about the morality of settlers on the frontier of Missouri as it does of Doniphan's legal prowess in defending such people. In a day when capital punishment was common, none of the men he defended ever faced the death penalty. No wonder accused criminals would gladly pay his outrageous fees. Doniphan expressed in later years regret for "helping so many guilty people to escape justice."[8]

Transcripts of his courtroom arguments are hard to find. Court clerks were not prone to make detailed transcriptions of the proceedings. Perhaps this is for the best. The absence of thorough records preserves the legacy and mystique that still surrounds Doniphan to this day. The only entirely preserved texts of his arguments are splattered with repetitive expletives that leave even the ardent historian questioning Doniphan's Southern gentility.

Missionaries to the Lamanites and Doniphan

At the time Doniphan was making a name for himself in the Fifth Judicial Circuit, Oliver Cowdery, Peter Whitmer Jr., Ziba Peterson, and Parley P. Pratt were making plans to journey from western New York to the borders of the Lamanites—a phrase understood to mean the line between Missouri and the American Indian territory—to share the gospel of Jesus Christ with American Indians.

"Emma Smith, and several other sisters" made their "necessary clothing" for the journey.[9] Other Saints gave the men food and copies of the Book of Mormon. In a spirit of rejoicing, the four men left western New York in October 1830 "to proclaim glad tidings of great joy" to American Indians residing fifteen hundred miles away on the westward borders of the United States.[10]

---

8   Launius, *Alexander William Doniphan*, 26.
9   Lavinia Fielding Anderson, ed., *Lucy's Book: A Critical Edition of Lucy Mack Smith's Family Memoir*, (Salt Lake City: Signature Books, 2001), 502–503.
10   Oliver Cowdery, "A Revelation unto Oliver, given September, 1830," *The Ohio Star* 2 no. 49 (December 8, 1831).

News of their travels was not kept secret. "The news of our coming," Parley P. Pratt wrote, "was soon noised abroad, and the news of the discovery of the Book of Mormon and the marvelous events connected with it."[11] Although the men faced "bitter cold, a blinding, swirling blur of snow" they trekked onward to reach Independence, Missouri, the farthest western settlement in the United States—the last outpost on the border of the Lamanites.[12]

Was it a coincidence that within weeks of their arrival, the Fifth Judicial Circuit held court in Independence or that Doniphan was in town? "I met Oliver Cowdery, John Whitmer, and Christian Whitmer, three of the Elders, in Independence, during the spring of 1831," Doniphan said. "Peter Whitmer was a tailor and I employed him to make me a suit of clothes."[13] (Doniphan was confused. Christian Whitmer was not with the missionaries traveling to the Lamanites.)

Little did Doniphan know that in the spring of 1831, a simple customer-tailor relationship with the first Latter-day Saints to ever step foot in Missouri was the beginning of what would propel him to the attention of society at large. His relationship with the Latter-day Saints would bring him more attention than all his previous cases or courtroom theatrics. It would put Doniphan in the limelight as a hero against a backdrop of unchecked hatred and bigotry.

A New Zion

Independence, Missouri, was the trailhead of the lucrative fur trade. Trappers and hunters alike paused in Independence before and after heading west on the Santa Fe Trail to Mexico. The trail held the promise of huge profits for trappers and hunters

---

11   Parley P. Pratt, *The Autobiography of Parley Parker Pratt* (Chicago: Law, King & Law, 1888), 35–36.

12   Eleanor Atkinson, "The Winter of the Deep Snow," in *Transactions of the Illinois State Historical Society for the Year 1909: Tenth Annual Meeting of the Society, Springfield, Ill., May 13–14, 1909* (Springfield: Illinois State Historical Library, 1910), 49.

13   "The Settlement of the Peculiar People in Jackson County and Subsequent Expulsion," *Kansas City Daily Journal* (June 12, 1881), quoted in Alexander Doniphan Committee, *The Will of Missouri*, 4.

willing to take risks. But only the brave or foolhardy were willing to travel on the trail. The stakes were high—a gamble between wealth and poverty and a race between life and death.

Besides the transient trail travelers, men from the Deep South were in Independence, pocketing a quick buck at the trailhead. The sights and sounds of the new South and the rugged frontier of western Missouri was a strange mix, but somehow the combination worked in the border town.

What didn't work in the town was the influx of Latter-day Saints from the Northern states. The Prophet Joseph Smith and his party arrived in Independence on July 14, 1831. In this last frontier, the Lord revealed that Missouri was "the land of promise, and the place for the city of Zion."[14] The Lord further revealed, "Behold, the place which is now called Independence is the center place; and the spot for the temple is lying westward, upon a lot which is not far from the courthouse."[15] The Lord told His Prophet Joseph that one reason for their coming to Independence was so that "you might be honored in laying the foundation, and in bearing record of the land upon which the Zion of God shall stand."[16]

The Prophet Joseph was so confident that Independence, Missouri, was the place of Zion, that on August 2, 1831, he had Sidney Rigdon dedicate the ground where the community of Zion was to be built.[17] During the dedicatory service, Rigdon asked the Latter-day Saints,

> "Do you receive this land for the land of your inheritance with thankful hearts, from the Lord?"
> Answer from all:—"We do."

---

14 D&C 57:2.
15 D&C 57:3.
16 D&C 58:7.
17 D&C 58:57.

"Do you pledge yourselves to keep the law of God in this land which you never have kept in your own lands?"

"We do."

"Do you pledge yourselves to see that others of your brethren who shall come hither do keep the laws of God?"

"We do."[18]

After offering a dedicatory prayer, Sidney Rigdon said, "I now pronounce this land consecrated and dedicated unto the Lord for a possession and inheritance for the Saints (in the name of Jesus Christ, having authority from Him). And for all the faithful servants of the Lord to the remotest ages of time. Amen."[19]

The Prophet Joseph then "laid a stone at the North east corner of the contemplated Temple in the name of the Lord Jesus of Nazareth."[20] Of this sacred event, he penned, "I proceeded to dedicate the spot for the Temple, a little west of Independence."[21] To Joseph, "it was a season of joy to those present, and afforded a glimpse of the future, which time will yet unfold to the satisfaction of the faithful."[22]

On August 4, 1831, the first Church conference was held in the land of Zion. During and after the conference, Joseph received revelations promising blessings to those "whose feet stand upon the land of Zion, who have obeyed my gospel."[23] From that time forward, the Saints began to journey to Missouri—their Zion. They came with the hope of a millennial society, even a New

18   Smith, *History of the Church*, 1:196.
19   F. Mark McKiernan and Roger D. Launius, eds., *An Early Latter Day Saint History: The Book of John Whitmer* (Independence, MO: Herald Publishing House, 1980), 79; punctuation and capitalization standardized.
20   John Whitmer, in History, 1831–circa 1847, 32, josephsmithpapers.org.
21   History, 1838–1856 [23 December 1805–30 August 1834], volume A-1, 137, josephsmithpapers.org.
22   History, 137.
23   D&C 59:3.

Jerusalem. They were given lands of inheritance and were called to live the sacred doctrines of the law of tithing and the law of consecration.

Was all well in their Zion-like society? Absolutely not. The slave-holding, slave-driving Southerners of Independence had tolerated the trappers and hunters thus far, for there was a profit to be made from them. But the Southerners could not and would not abide Northerners talking of Independence as Zion or building a millennial society there. To those from the South, such foolery was an affront to their way of life. They did not like the Northern Protestant work ethic that defied the institution of slavery. They could not abide white men scratching in the fields.

Tensions mounted as the newcomers spoke openly of lands of inheritance and their Zion-like society. When they tried to convert the Southerners to their ways and religion, civility was all but gone. The Missourians wanted to speak of slaves, of profits, and of taming more of the frontier. But before long, the profit element in fur, tobacco, and hemp moved to the backburner as their hatred of the Northerners, who had a strange religion and who were putting down roots in Independence, dominated conversations. It was then that Doniphan moved from Lexington to the border town of Liberty and made his stand.

CHAPTER THREE
The Move to Liberty, Missouri

DAVID RICE ATCHISON WAS A mirror of Alexander Doniphan, although he was a year older and not as attractive to the ladies. Atchison stood over six feet tall and was "a jovial man with simple tastes" and sympathies that often turned to the common man.[1] He had a flair for courtroom theatrics that began at the University of Transylvania when he and fellow classmate Jefferson Davis, later president of the Confederate States from 1861–1865, entertained paying crowds. In August 1830, Atchison had moved from his home state of Kentucky to Missouri, unfettered by familial ties. He set up his law practice in the courthouse square in Liberty. Being an energetic orator, he didn't disappoint courtroom spectators or juries.

The difference between Atchison and Doniphan was that Atchison settled in Liberty, a town of about three hundred people, whereas Doniphan settled in Lexington, a vibrant community of twenty-five hundred inhabitants. Liberty, the seat of Clay County, was close to the state's western boundary and was not a busy transshipment hub like Lexington or Independence. Liberty was more of a quiet suburb that attracted a gentler society from

---

1 William E. Parrish, "David Rice Atchison of Missouri, Border Politician," *University of Missouri Studies* 34, no. 1 (Columbia: University of Missouri Press, 1961), quoted in Kathleen Bird, "Pick a Side: Doniphan's Role in Missouri's Loyalty to the Union," quoted in Alexander Doniphan Committee, *The Will of Missouri,* 117.

the South, though the town was projected to become a major outpost—a more important transshipment destination than even Lexington.

Atchison liked Doniphan from the moment they met. Atchison could see himself working well with Doniphan and being his friend. He came up with several reasons why they should be law partners and why Doniphan would find life in Liberty exciting. It was a hard sell at first but never a closed topic when the two young lawyers met in the Fifth Judicial Circuit District. After weighing the pros and cons for months, Doniphan agreed to join Atchison in Liberty. In May 1833, at age twenty-five, Doniphan packed up his law office and belongings and moved about forty miles to Liberty, not realizing that this Western town would be his home for the next thirty years.

The relationship between Doniphan and Atchison was more than amicable—they were like brothers. They hunted wild game from dawn to dusk and played cards with the seedy parts of society as if the prize money were a fortune. In taverns, they swapped stories, bet on horse races, and gambled as if money meant nothing. When Atchison organized the Liberty Blues Militia, he named himself captain and Doniphan, of course, his first officer. The Liberty Blues "drilled three times per year, marched around in the sun for a while and then settled down for a picnic and not just a little drink."[2]

One wintry evening when Doniphan and Atchison were playing cards with a few ruffians, a local sheriff caught them betting "a large sum of money"—twenty-five cents. Indignant over such extravagant betting, the sheriff arrested the twosome and had them stand trial. Judge Amos Rees, who later was a partner of Doniphan at the famed Richmond hearing, fined the two lawyers $5.25 each for breaking the law. Doniphan thought he and Atchison might have been more successful in their law practice had they stayed in their offices more and spent

2 John Dilingham, "Civil War Roundtable: Alexander W. Doniphan," quoted in Alexander Doniphan Committee, *The Will of Missouri*, 241.

less time in the woods and at parties. But there was more to life than the law, and these two young men were adventurous enough to find it.

As their partnership began, Atchison had more law cases than Doniphan. Atchison also received greater remuneration for his legal services. Doniphan had kept the doors open in his legal practice at Lexington by charging small fees. Seeing Atchison's success, Doniphan wanted a bigger piece of the legal pie. He rationalized that he had paid his dues as a young attorney and could now demand higher wages for his service. Atchison pushed every variety of legal work to Doniphan, trying to ensure he would stay in Liberty.

Before long, clients were seeking Doniphan's counsel on delayed shipments of hogs, land titles, legal rights to slaves, etc. However, none of these legal maneuverings were as exciting to Doniphan as defending accused criminals. None of the maneuverings garnered him much of a reputation in Liberty or filled a courtroom, and the mundane work was not to his liking. Atchison was content to make a buck off businessmen; Doniphan was not.

Atchison had "a clear logical mind; had studied law well, and kept up with his profession by constant reading, when he was not engaged actively out of doors. . . . The position he took in any case he sustained with ability, and when he was on the right side, he rarely failed of success."[3] Doniphan was not of the same mindset. He had a rare talent for criminal law—the law that captured fear and imagination. The horror of brazen thefts, rape, and murder meant drama in the courtroom—it was what Doniphan did best, and Atchison knew it. Atchison said,

---

3   William E. Parrish, "David Rice Atchison of Missouri, Border Politician," *University of Missouri Studies* 34, no. 1 (Columbia: University of Missouri Press, 1961), quoted in Kathleen Bird, "Pick a Side: Doniphan's Role in Missouri's Loyalty to the Union," quoted in Alexander Doniphan Committee, *The Will of Missouri*, 117; Launius, *Alexander William Doniphan*, 13.

> I was familiar with the city of Washington in my early manhood. I knew all the great men of our country in the earlier days—Clay, Webster, Calhoun, John Quincy Adams . . . and others. I have presided in the United States Senate when Clay, Webster, and Calhoun sat before me. I knew Aleck Doniphan familiarly, intimately, since 1830, and I tell you, sir, when he was in his prime I heard him climb higher than any of them.[4]

Biographer Robert D. Launius concurred:

> [Doniphan] argued plausibly, even his supporters said, but rarely deeply. He could make a case with grand eloquence, punctuated with flourishing metaphors and similes. . . . If accused of a serious crime, no one could better address a jury than Doniphan. In frontier Missouri, where court was even more an adventure in theater than today, the oratorical display of attorneys served well, and Doniphan had that skill in abundance.[5]

Unfortunately, Doniphan's combative, theatrical approach to the courtroom brought on emotional and even mental problems. Although Doniphan was an imposing, almost towering man, he suffered from health issues that could be described but not explained to the satisfaction of anyone, especially not to himself. He would throw himself into a criminal case and afterwards be completely exhausted. In one case, the physician, who was as baffled as Doniphan, prescribed bed rest for weeks.

In spite of an emotional malady that took a toll on his energy and required complete quiet on doctor's orders, Doniphan never

---

4   Gregory Maynard, "Alexander William Doniphan, the Forgotten Man from Missouri," (master's thesis, Brigham Young University, 1973), 114.
5   Launius, *Alexander William Doniphan*, 26–27.

publicly lamented his malady. He looked for no excuse. In the courtroom, he was out to win for himself and his client. His only public regret was "having been the cause of so many scoundrels going unhung."[6] In later years, when his energy was spent and there was little in reserve for him to climb out of bed or face the next case, Doniphan recalled that "this type of work was for the young."[7] But in the 1830s, he was one of the young and would not allow his problems to slow his drive or legal reputation.

Latter-day Saints Hire Attorneys

By the summer of 1833, Southerners in Independence had denounced Mormonism as a strange and threatening religion and its Northern adherents as unwanted. Southerners had no qualms ridiculing or intimidating Latter-day Saints, be it a man, woman, or child. A few Saints tried to stand up for their rights against their Southern neighbors, but little came of it. Southerners boasted that they could drive the Mormons out of the county without a backlash.

When word of the persecutors' boasts reached Joseph Smith in Kirtland, Ohio, he counseled his followers in Independence to rise above retaliation and renew their resolve to build New Jerusalem—a Zion-like community—in spite of outward challenges. Encouraged by his words and with defiant determination, Latter-day Saints clutched hammers, shovels, and spades and went about building the prophesied community. Ironically, in a frontier settlement whose name, Independence, heralds man's inalienable rights, the Saints' efforts were hampered on every side.

Latter-day Saint leaders drafted a letter to the Democratic Missouri governor, Daniel Dunklin, asking for help from the mob-like element who called for the Saints' removal from Independence. Governor Dunklin replied, "I have no regard for the Mormons, as a separate people; & have an utter contempt

---

6 Raymond W. Settle, "Colonel Doniphan—Symbol of Pioneer Americanism," *William Jewell College Bulletin* 20, no. 7 (1947): quoted in Maynard, *Alexander William Doniphan*, 77.

7 Launius, *Alexander William Doniphan*, 27.

for them as a religious sect; while on the other hand I have much regard for the people of Jackson County, both personally and politically; they are, many of them, my personal friends, and nearly all of them are very staunch Democrats."[8] Wanting to pass the buck and keep his hands unsullied in the rising conflict between the Latter-day Saints and their neighbors, Governor Dunklin suggested the Saints take their complaints to the courts. In other words, turn from the executive branch to the judicial branch and leave him out of it.

For all intents and purposes, Governor Dunklin washed his hands of the problem and kicked it under the rug, hoping it would go away. He suggested to the Saints, "The judge of your circuit is a conservator of the peace. If an affidavit is made before him, by any of you, that your lives are threatened, and you believed them in danger, it would be his duty to have the offenders apprehended and bind them to keep the peace."[9]

In the fall of 1833, perceiving the judicial branch as the next best step, Latter-day Saint leaders in Independence approached four attorneys—Alexander Doniphan, David Rice Atchison, William T. Wood, and Amos Rees. Each attorney was in the Independence courthouse during the Fifth Judicial Circuit Court, waiting their turn to represent their respective clients. Quickly recognizing the number of complaints the Latter-day Saints were willing to enter, the attorneys saw dollar signs and agreed to represent them. In their letter of October 28, 1833, they proposed a fee for their legal services:

> We are now laboring under all the disadvantages
> of an engagement, without any of its advantages;
> it therefore becomes us to know, whether we can
> agree as to the fee, or not. . . . We have been doing a
> practice here [in Liberty], among these people, to a

8 Dunklin to Joel Haden, August 14, 1832, quoted in Launius, *Alexander William Doniphan*, 14–15.
9 History, 1838–1856, volume A-1 [23 December 1805–30 August 1834], 363–364, josephsmithpapers.org.

considerable extent, and, by this engagement, we
must expect to loose the greatest part of it, which
will be to all of us a considerable loss; besides that
the amount involved must be very considerable,
and the amount involved must be generally the
criterion of the fee. Taking all these matters into
consideration, we propose to you to bring all the
suits you may want brought, and attend to them
jointly throughout, for the sum of two hundred
and fifty dollars each, making for all four of us
the sum of one thousand dollars. This may seem
to be a large sum for a fee for Lawyers in this
country, but the circumstances here involved
make it necessary. . . . If this proposal suits, you
will please execute notes, and send them to us:
and if not agree to apprise us by letter immediately, for we can be engaged on the opposite side
in all probability. We prefer to bring your suits, as
we have been threatened by the mob we wish to
shew them we disregard their empty bravadoes.[10]

On October 29, 1833, Bishop Edward Partridge, who held
the financial purse strings of the Church in Independence, agreed
to the exorbitant fee and promised that within six months the
four attorneys would be paid.

The Mob Element Reacts
The golden opportunity for Doniphan to be in the spotlight,
the opportunity that opened his door wide to embrace fame was
when he agreed to be one of four attorneys to represent the Latter-
day Saints. He agreed to seek justice for the persecuted minority,
but he never accepted their belief that they were "persecuted solely
because of their religion."[11] Doniphan thought the issue had

10   History, 365.
11   Launius, *Alexander William Doniphan*, 14.

much more to do with North and South—a hotbed topic that did not bode well for Northerners in Missouri.

When the mob element in Jackson County learned that attorneys had been retained and that the Saints were determined to stay their ground in Independence, build up Zion, and create a millennial society, violence erupted. On the eve of October 31, 1833, a lawless mob unroofed and destroyed ten houses in a small Latter-day Saint settlement that bordered the Big Blue River. On November 4, when the same mob began to destroy other property along the Big Blue, the Saints fought back in a bloody skirmish on the east side of the river. Reacting to the news of injury and death, on November 5, well-armed Southern men from all parts of the county converged on the Latter-day Saints in Independence, demanding that they surrender their arms, abandon their property, and run for their lives out of the county.

"All my property was scattered to the four winds, tools and all for pretended claims, where I owed not one cent justly," wrote Levi Hancock.[12] Joseph Knight tried to preserve his property from pillage and destruction: "We calmly submitted to the numerous indignities *heaped* upon us . . . [and] made many concessions to the mob in hope of pacifying them, but it was useless."[13] Parley P. Pratt wrote, "My house was . . . burned, and my fruit trees and improvements destroyed or plundered. In short, every member of the society was driven from the county, and fields of corn were ravaged and destroyed; stacks of wheat burned, household goods plundered, and improvements and every kind of property destroyed."[14]

Rather than defend themselves, Latter-day Saints fled from the ruthless mobs to the banks of the Missouri River. They crossed the river to Clay County, where they were welcomed with restrained compassion. Unfortunately, however, there was a limit

---

12   Levi Hancock, *Autobiography* (1803–1836), typescript, 50.

13   Newell Knight, "Newell Knight's Journal," *Classic Experiences and Adventures* (Salt Lake City: Bookcraft, 1969), 97; italics added.

14   Parley P. Pratt, *The Autobiography of Parley Parker Pratt* (Chicago: Law, King & Law, 1888), 110.

to the hospitality citizens of Clay were willing to offer, especially when their cousins in Jackson had taken to arms.

As Doniphan reflected on what happened to cause such an affront to life, liberty, and the inalienable right to pursue happiness, he said,

> [The Latter-day Saints] were northern people, who, on account of their declining to own slaves and their denunciation of the system of slavery, were termed "Free Soilers." The majority of them were intelligent, industrious and law-abiding citizens, but there were some ignorant, simple minded fanatics among them, whom the prophet said would steal. . . . They established a newspaper at Independence called the Morning and Evening Star, edited by W.W. Phelps, in which they published their peculiar tenets and pretended revelations in which they set forth that they had been sent to Jackson County by divine Providence and that they, as a church were to possess the whole of the country, which then embraced what is now Jackson, Cass, and Bates Counties. . . . This of course caused hard feelings between them and the people of the county, but I think the real objections to the Mormons were their denunciation of slavery, and the objections slave holders had to having so large a settlement of anti-slavery people in their midst, and also to their acquiring such a large amount of land, which then belonged to the government, and subject to pre-emption. From these and other causes, a very bitter feeling was engendered between the Mormons and citizens.[15]

15   "The Settlement of the Peculiar People in Jackson County and Subsequent Expulsion," quoted in Alexander Doniphan Committee, *The Will of Missouri*, 4–5.

Doniphan and Atchison Represent the Latter-day Saints

Doniphan and Atchison took the leading roles in defending the Saints, although the other two attorneys were on the payroll. The two young lawyers met with Missouri Attorney General Robert W. Wells, who led them to believe that the state of Missouri would restore the Latter-day Saints to their property in Jackson and send troops to ensure the Saints' protection. Wells told Doniphan in a letter, "If they decide to be replaced in their property, that is, their houses in Jackson county, an adequate force will be sent forthwith to effect that object."[16]

Judge John F. Ryland of the Fifth Judicial Circuit was not an unobservant bystander to the atrocities in Jackson County. He viewed what had happened to the Latter-day Saints in Jackson as unacceptable to free men in a civilized society. He demanded an investigation into the matter of why US citizens should be forced at gunpoint to abandon their property to lawless mobs. He expressed a willingness to convene court in Jackson County anytime. In other words, he wanted his schedule to be interrupted if necessary so the matter could be carefully considered. He wrote, "It is a disgrace to the State, for such acts to happen within its limits."[17]

Doniphan and Atchison reviewed with Attorney General Wells the feasibility of holding a non-partial and non-explosive court hearing in Independence. They concluded the case should be postponed, giving time for the heated situation between the Southerners and the Mormons to cool down. A court date was set for February 24, 1834, in Independence.

Doniphan and Atchison worked for weeks in the winter of 1834 to find favorable witnesses willing to cross the Missouri River to testify against the mob element. A. Sidney Gilbert wrote to Governor Dunklin, "It is my opinion from present

---

16 Wells to A. W. Doniphan and David R. Atchison, November 21, 1833, quoted in Launius, *Alexander William Doniphan*, 18.

17 History, 1838–1856, volume A-1 [23 December 1805–30 August 1834], 383, josephsmithpapers.org.

appearances, that not one fourth of the witnesses of our people, can be prevailed upon to go into Jackson county to testify."[18] On December 6, 1833, Doniphan and Atchison drafted a letter to Governor Daniel Dunklin on behalf of the exiled Saints in Clay:

> In behalf of our society, which is so scattered and suffering, we, your petitioners, ask aid and assistance of your Excellency, that we may be restored to our lands, houses, and property, and protected in them by the militia of the state. . . . We ask that our men may be organized into companies of Jackson Guards, and be furnished with arms by the state, to assist in maintaining their rights against the unhallowed power of the mob of Jackson county. . . . We wish a court of inquiry instituted, to investigate the whole matter of the mob against the "Mormons."[19]

While waiting for the governor to reply, several attempts were made to reconcile differences between the Latter-day Saints and the residents of Jackson. At one such reconciliation meeting, Doniphan sat quietly listening to what had become a heated argument. Not willing to sit any longer, he stood up and said in a shrill, loud voice that he advocated the rights of the Latter-day Saints and disdained mob violence as uncivilized. "The Mormons have armed themselves," he said in reference to Zion's Camp. "If they don't fight they are cowards. I love to hear that they have brethren coming to their assistance. Greater love can no man show, than he who lays down his life for his brethren."[20] Some in the courtroom had not heard of Zion's Camp. When the number of Latter-day Saint men marching to Independence was exaggerated,

18 History, 415.
19 W. W. Phelps et al., to Daniel Dunklin, December 6, 1833, quoted in Launius, *Alexander William Doniphan*, 17.
20 History, 1838–1856, volume A-1 [23 December 1805–30 August 1834], 493, josephsmithpapers.org.

palpable fear replaced anger. When anxiety creeped from one man to another, the meeting was over.

By the time the February 24, 1834, Fifth Judicial Circuit Court was held in Independence, Governor Dunklin, who had washed his hands of the matter months before, was interested in the proceedings and knew that armed men were marching towards Independence. Dunklin issued orders activating the Liberty Blues Militia to ensure the judicial proceeding would be peaceful. When Atchison was called to arms as the captain of the Liberty Blues Militia, he was unable to defend the Saints. Instead, he led about fifty citizen-soldiers to the Independence Courthouse Square to provide needed security and military strength. According to biographer Roger D. Launius, "Although Atchison had to recuse himself from the legal proceedings, his presence ensured more stability than if an unproven commander and unit had been present."[21]

Judge Ryland sat on the bench. Attorney General Wells was in the audience. A mob assembled outside the courthouse. Even though the Liberty Blues protected witnesses ready to testify, and the defense attorneys were in their place, Judge Ryland postponed the trial. Was the postponement due to fear of the mob element? Yes! Not even the judge wanted to be caught in the crossfire between Southern agitators and the Mormons. Newel Knight said, "All hope of a criminal prosecution was at an end. Thus were the officers of the civil law, even when supported by the military, awed by a mob, and the great promises of the governor and judge Ryland fell to the ground, and the strong arm of justice became weak and fell powerless to her side."[22]

Other attempts were made to put Latter-day Saints back on their lands, including a change of venue for the court proceedings, but nothing worked. The efforts of Doniphan were largely fruitless. Latter-day Saints did not fault him, however; they knew the young attorney was no match for the men in high standing in

21 Launius, *Alexander William Doniphan*, 19.
22 Newel Knight, "Autobiography," 90, quoted in Launius, *Alexander William Doniphan*, 19.

Independence—at least, not yet. Mobs and men of means had power and influence. The power of the pocketbook spoke louder than justice.

The Issue of Latter-day Saints in Clay County

By the fall of 1834, there was little talk of property claims and claims of abuse in Jackson County. Latter-day Saints, who had settled in a waiting posture in Clay, now spoke of permanency in towns like Liberty. As for Doniphan, his legal counsel for the Saints was needed on occasion, but he was free to expand his interests.

Not one to sit idle or wait for opportunity, Doniphan refashioned himself into an attorney with a diversified portfolio. He purchased large tracts of farmland in Clay County and a city lot in Liberty on which he planned to erect a Southern mansion. He built up a sizable legal practice and took a flirting interest in politics, espoused by the Whig Party. The Whigs promoted a middle-of-the-road, steady-as-she-goes platform; in other words, they took a "don't steady the ark" approach.

Unavoidably, the question of Mormons surfaced. This time it was in Liberty, not Independence or Jackson County. Fearful Southern residents of Liberty claimed the Latter-day Saints were "flocking [to Liberty] faster than ever and making great talk [of] what they would do. A letter from Ohio [where Joseph Smith lived] Shows plainly that they intended to Emigrate here til they outnumber us. Then they would rule the Co[u]ntry at pleasure."[23]

On June 16, 1836, at the Liberty Courthouse Square, the question of Mormons and their strange religion was debated before an audience of about a thousand residents. Samuel C. Owens, who had been in the mob that drove the Saints out of Jackson County, addressed the crowd, urging residents to drive the Mormons from Clay County. He claimed to know the power

---

23   A. Wilson and Emelia Wilson to Brother and Sister, July 4, 1836, quoted in Launius, *Alexander William Doniphan*, 38. Third set of brackets in the original.

of lawless mobs and that the Mormons would cower against the mob element and move on. It was then that Doniphan,

> who had been a listener and thought their prop-
> osition rather too stringent, arose and began to
> shove up his sleeves, (his manner when a little
> warmed up), and commenced his remarks in a
> rather excited tone, when the chairman or some-
> one called him to order, saying he was giving too
> strong vent to his feelings; that it was calculated
> to raise an excitement in the crowd, whose feel-
> ings were then almost ready to boil over. The
> Colonel pulled his sleeve up a little higher, and
> told him, "that was what he got up for—to give
> vent to his feelings."[24]

Doniphan spoke with eloquence on the "right of citizen and individual liberty, with individual responsibility, and [he personally] was opposed to . . . mob violence; was in favor of law and order; the law was made for the punishment of evil doers, and to protect the law-abiding, and should be strictly enforced."[25] The citizens calmed down, for his was the voice of reason, the Southern drawl that compelled listeners to thoughtful consideration.

But the issue was far from resolved. On June 29, 1836, in the Liberty courthouse, Doniphan and Clay County leaders met to discuss a solution to the Mormon problem that did not include forcing the Saints from Clay, destroying their property, or raising a lawless mob. After heavy discussion that seemed to circle rather than address the issue, county leaders agreed to a few pointed resolutions. They resolved, "We therefore, in a spirit of frank and friendly kindness, do advise them to seek a home where they may obtain large and separate bodies of land, and

24   Judge Joseph Thorp, *Early Days in the West*, 80, quoted in Launius, *Alexander William Doniphan*, 38.
25   Thorp, *Early Days in the West*, 80, quoted in Launius, *Alexander William Doniphan*, 38.

have a community of their own." County leaders resolved "that [Mormon] emigration cease, and cease immediately, as nothing else can or will allay for a moment, the deep excitement that is now unhappily agitating this community."[26] The resolutions were straightforward—there was no hidden agenda, no secrets. "Get out and don't come back" was the bottom line.

Fearful of a continuation of the nightmarish scenes of hostilities in Jackson, Latter-day Saint leaders turned to Doniphan. He was the linchpin who had reason to support both sides. The Saints wanted a place where they could be left alone to live their religion. The residents of Clay County wanted nothing more than to have the Saints move to that place—any place but Clay.

---

26   "Public Meeting," *Latter Day Saints' Messenger and Advocate* 2, no. 2, (August 1836): 354–355.

CHAPTER FOUR
A Public Figure

DONIPHAN'S FIRST FORAY IN THE political arena was to replace his law partner, David Atchison, who decided not to run again for the state legislature. With Atchison's support, Doniphan was elected to the Missouri House of Representatives by a large margin. He began his service in the Ninth General Assembly of the state of Missouri on November 21, 1836.

Even though Doniphan was a newcomer in the legislature and protocol demanded he sit back and learn from seasoned legislators, sitting back was not his way. The legislative body hardly had a chance to listen to proposed legislation before he had an opinion ready to express. Before long, Doniphan had garnered a reputation of going against the grain. If a particular bit of legislation was an unpopular stance, Doniphan backed it. If there was a fight for an underdog, Doniphan didn't mind being on the bottom of the pile. He wanted to be a politician like Henry Clay. Of the Whig senator, Doniphan said, "I worshipped Clay as no man but him was ever worshipped by his followers."[1]

During his two years in office, Doniphan supported annexing the Platte region, which added northwest counties to

---

1 William B. McGroarty, ed., "Letters from Alexander W. Doniphan," v. 24, no.1 (October 1929), 27.

the state. When newly elected Governor Lilburn W. Boggs wanted a state bank that paid paper money on demand, Doniphan voted for chartering the Bank of the State of Missouri. He also voted in favor of incorporating fourteen insurance companies who promised to insure steamers on the Missouri and Mississippi Rivers. He fostered the passage of laws on American Indian affairs, slavery, and on manufacturing and mining enterprises. In his votes, a pattern emerged—he rarely considered a Democratic proposal. When a resolution was called for to give the outgoing US president, Andrew Jackson, a vote of "respect, esteem and best wishes for his future happiness at his retirement," Doniphan voted, "Nay."[2]

Doniphan Speaks Up for the Saints

The most impressive parts of his two years in office were when Doniphan spoke up in behalf of the hated Mormons, one more example of his willingness to take a stand for a minority. He told members of the general assembly about the hostile situation in his county and introduced a bill to organize a county specifically designated and set aside for the Latter-day Saints. He proposed that the county be named after Captain Matthew Caldwell, a commander in the Revolutionary War and a friend of his father.

Opponents to the bill argued that settlements dominated by Mormons would hinder, rather than promote, prosperity and future emigration. They claimed that if Mormons had a county of their own, it would disturb the peace. They cited examples of problems in Jackson County and Clay County to verify their assumptions. Due to strong opposition against the bill, the intended borders of Caldwell County were reduced by more than half with a proposed second county to the north, named Daviess.

Doniphan opposed carving a second county out of Caldwell County and said to William W. Phelps, "I did not succeed as you wished or as you might have expected, in fixing the boundaries

2   *Journal of the House of Representatives . . . First Session of the Ninth General Assembly*, 373, quoted in Launius, *Alexander William Doniphan*, 41.

of your county. . . . I was forced to report a bill making two counties . . . instead of one. In time, I hope you may add to its [the county's] limits, when prejudices have subsided and reason and common sense have again assumed the helm."[3]

On December 23, 1836, the bill to organize the counties of Caldwell and Daviess passed the House and, four days later, the Senate. Governor Lilburn W. Boggs signed the bill into law on December 29, 1836.

The bill offered a window of hope, a temporary solution to Latter-day Saints, who feared the same hostilities that erupted in Jackson were at their doorsteps in Clay. The bill did not specify which of the two counties the Latter-day Saints were entitled to settle. Church leaders chose Caldwell County. The sentiment among the Missourians was, "If the Mormons are willing to go into that prairie country and settle, let them have it."[4]

The prairie land of Caldwell had few attractions. The land was flat. There was poor irrigation, poor soil, and no rivers. Yet that didn't stop Latter-day Saints from moving to the area. Doniphan wrote, "The new county filled up very rapidly and they made great progress in agricultural and other improvements."[5]

Doniphan knew the move to Caldwell was a bandage, not a solution to the problems facing the Mormons. As a result, he was less inclined to accept compliments for pushing the bill through to create the Mormon county.

Marriage

Doniphan did not run for reelection in 1838 or receive an appointment to serve in the Tenth General Assembly of the state of Missouri. He hadn't lost interest in politics or his desire to be like Henry Clay and champion the cause of minorities.

---

3   A. W. Doniphan to W. W. Phelps, January 8, 1837, quoted in Launius, *Alexander William Doniphan*, 40.

4   Andrew Jenson, *The Historical Record* (1888), 689.

5   "The Settlement for the Peculiar People in Jackson County and Subsequent Expulsion," quoted in Alexander Doniphan Committee, *The Will of Missouri*, 6–7.

But there were more important matters of a personal nature that Doniphan wanted to pursue. In 1838, twenty-nine-year-old Doniphan was a much sought-after bachelor. No doubt, many a woman would have chased him down if given the opportunity. He was not only a striking figure but also a public figure. He had a thriving law firm and was a courtroom favorite in the Fifth Judicial Circuit. He owned 160 acres of rich farmland outright in Clay County and was poised to purchase additional acreage.

Of all the young woman who could have captured his attention, it was Elizabeth "Jane" Thornton, the eldest daughter of John Thornton, who outshone them all. John Thornton gave Doniphan permission to call on his sixteen-year-old daughter. On Jane's seventeenth birthday, December 21, 1837, at the Old School Baptist Church in Liberty, Alexander William Doniphan wed Jane Thornton. Oliver Perry Moss of Maysville, Kentucky—and one of Doniphan's close friends—wed Jane's sister, Caroline Thornton, on the same day in a double-marriage ceremony.

Doniphan wrote of his bride,

> My wife was a lovely woman; I married her the day she was seventeen; I was glad she had no more education than the Common Schools of this frontier country then afforded; I desired to educate her myself—to form her mind and tastes—I was young, liberally educated, and energetic. I never read a book to myself (other than a Law work) during more than thirty years of married life; I read them all to her and with her, she often relieving me.[6]

D. C. Allen, a close friend and legal associate, said of their marriage:

6 Doniphan to Emma Doniphan, 1875, quoted in Launius, *Alexander William Doniphan*, 41–42.

It was a perfect union of heart and intellect. She was a highly intellectual, cultivated woman, and her grace of manner and charm in conversation made her a delight of society. Save when public duty or business imperatively demanded it, he and she were constantly united. At home or abroad they were together. They were both insatiable readers, and their evenings in literature will always stir delightful thoughts in the memories of their friends. He knew and loved no place like home, and neither the mystery of lodges nor the joviality of clubs had any power to draw him thence.[7]

To those who knew her, Jane was "a child, wife, parent, and a friend of the poor and humble, she discharged a Christian's duty."[8]

The newlyweds resided at 124 North Main Street in Liberty, Missouri.

Doniphan relished his new role as husband and enjoyed familial relations with the Thorntons, in many ways the "First Family of Liberty." Although there were causes to address, criminals to defend, and properties to buy, Doniphan was content to be in the company of Jane. Theirs was a marriage of happiness and mutual respect.

Less than a year after their wedding, Jane gave birth to their firstborn son, John Thornton Doniphan—named for her father—on September 18, 1838. It was a time of great rejoicing in their family.

The Call to Arms

After less than a year of marriage, Doniphan became concerned over rising tensions between the Latter-day Saints and Southerners in northern Missouri. To him, it was just a matter of

---

7   D. C. Allen, quoted in Launius, *Alexander William Doniphan*, 41.
8   Fairview Cemetery (Liberty, Missouri), Elizabeth Jane Thornton headstone inscription.

time before a violent conflict broke out. He knew that in spite of his marital bliss, he would not sit idly by when there would surely be bloodshed.

From Doniphan's perspective, events leading up to the Mormon War began in the summer of 1838, a few months before the birth of his son. He placed the blame on Joseph Smith, who had arrived in northern Missouri and had orchestrated the settling of Adam-ondi-Ahman—

> [The Mormons in Caldwell County] continued to live prosperously and tranquilly until the summer of 1838, when Joseph Smith came out from Ohio and soon after [the Mormons] commenced forming a settlement in Davis County, which, under their agreement, they had no right to do. This occasioned difficulties with the citizens of Davis County, and in September, 1838, a large number of citizens of Davis and adjoining counties collected with arms in the Mormon settlement called "Adam-ondi-Ahman," in Davis [*sic*] county.
>
> The Mormons also gathered at the same point, and I, being at that time brigadier general of the western division of Missouri, was sent by Gov[enor] Boggs with a regiment of Clay County militia to prevent a collision, which after being there one week, I was able to do, and left them apparently harmonious, the Mormons agreeing that they would return to Caldwell County as soon as they could take care of their crops, etc. . . . About one month after this new difficulties arose between the citizens and Mormons, from what causes I never knew, which culminated in the Mormons burning

and sacking the Gentile towns of Millport and Gallatin, then very small villages.[9]

In Doniphan's view, the Saints were the aggressors and responsible for bringing upon themselves the Mormon War. Of course, Latter-day Saints did not agree with Doniphan's perception of the events. To them, it stemmed from the fight at the polls in Gallatin and the illegal actions by the state of Missouri to confine Mormons to Caldwell County.

The difference in perception was hard to overcome. Doniphan tried to mitigate feelings and slow down the public outcry with techniques that had worked for him in the courtroom. Few wanted theatrics when the call for war was sounding in every ear. Doniphan said, "A few days after this a battle took place on the line between Caldwell and Ray Counties between the Mormons, under the command of Capt. Patton and the citizens of Ray County, under command of Capt. Bogart in which two Ray County citizens and several Mormons, including Capt. Patton, were killed."[10]

By this juncture, there was no turning back for either side. The cry for war was heard throughout northern Missouri.

With such an impressive title as brigadier general, it is little wonder that stories, and nothing more than stories, began to circulate of Doniphan explaining to Joseph Smith that a military force of eight hundred soldiers was marching from Carroll to Daviess County to expel Mormons from Adam-ondi-Ahman and of Doniphan advising Joseph to defend the town. Doniphan decried the stories as nothing more than falsehoods, but few wanted to hear the truth when every man was reaching for his gun.

Although accounts vary as to the facts and place of events that led to the Mormon War, none deny that on October 27, 1838,

9   "The Settlement of the Peculiar People in Jackson County and Subsequent Expulsion," quoted in Alexander Doniphan Committee, *The Will of Missouri*, 7.
10   "The Settlement of the Peculiar People in Jackson County and Subsequent Expulsion," quoted in Alexander Doniphan Committee, *The Will of Missouri*, 7.

Governor Lilburn W. Boggs issued the following order: "The Mormons must be treated as enemies and must be exterminated or driven from the state, if necessary for the public good. Their outrages are beyond all description."[11] The governor next mobilized local militias to put down the Mormon uprising.

Doniphan wrote, "Gen. [David] Atchison . . . then major general of Northwest Missouri ordered me to raise a regiment of militia from Clay, Clinton, and Platte Counties. I did so, and proceeded at once to the battleground."[12] When his militia, numbering about three hundred citizen-soldiers, reached Ray County, Doniphan received orders "to take command of all the forces and remain in Ray County until the arrival of Gen. [John B.] Clark [of Howard County] with the state troops."[13]

For eleven days, Brigadier General Doniphan and his troops were in the field discharging the governor's demands. During this period, General David Atchison was relieved of his military duty due to expressing sympathy for the maligned Latter-day Saints. His command was turned over to Major General Samuel Lucas. Doniphan thought of also resigning his post. He had the same sympathetic leanings toward the Mormons. He also did not believe Governor Boggs had the power of office to issue an extermination order. Had he "not been persuaded by General Atchison and others that by remaining [he] might save the effusion of blood," Doniphan would never have agreed to stay on the battlefield.[14]

An Eyewitness to Betrayal

"I went on to Far West," Doniphan wrote. He and his citizen-soldiers arrived in the afternoon of October 30 in the city of the Saints. There he found

11   Governor Lilburn W. Boggs to Major General John B. Clark, October 27, 1838, quoted in Launius, *Alexander William Doniphan*, 57.
12   "The Settlement of the Peculiar People in Jackson County and Subsequent Expulsion," quoted in Alexander Doniphan Committee, *The Will of Missouri*, 7–8.
13   "The Settlement of the Peculiar People in Jackson County and Subsequent Expulsion," quoted in Alexander Doniphan Committee, *The Will of Missouri*, 8.
14   Doniphan to Major B. Holladay, April 5, 1850, quoted in Launius, *Alexander William Doniphan*, 58.

all the Mormon forces were assembled. . . . I
opened negotiations with the Mormons by going up to their lines in person . . . the Mormons
gave up their arms and turned over to me such
men as had violated the laws of the land. . . .
It has been said that in the treaty I made with
the Mormons, I stipulated that they must leave
the State, under penalty of annihilation if they
refused to do so. This is utterly untrue as I made
no such stipulation.[15]

Doniphan's words and actions were misconstrued and
exaggerated. It angered him, but no one was listening to reason.
Rumors found a ready audience, not truth. Fear trumped logic
as militias brandished their weapons. Traitors and profiteers saw
advantages in fear. They watched Latter-day Saints run to the
wilderness before the criminals began stealing from abandoned
homes. Atrocities followed, but not before a devastating betrayal.

Doniphan was not surprised when, on October 31, Joseph
Smith and other Latter-day Saint leaders were betrayed by
the Mormon leader of the Caldwell County Militia, George
Hinkle. Joseph Smith did not share Doniphan's viewpoint. The
betrayal was not expected, nor was the treatment Joseph Smith
and other Church leaders received at the hands of riotous men
posing as citizens-soldiers under the command of General
Samuel Lucas. Joseph wrote,

Instead of being treated with that respect which
is due from one Citizen to another, we were
taken as Prisoners of War, and were treated with
the utmost contempt. The officers would not
converse with us, and the soldiers, almost to a
man, insulted us as much as they felt disposed,

---

15   "The Settlement of the Peculiar People in Jackson County and Subsequent Expulsion,"
quoted in Alexander Doniphan Committee, *The Will of Missouri*, 8.

breathing out threats against me and my companions.

I cannot begin to tell the scene which I there witnessed. The Loud cries and yells of more than one thousand voices, which rent the air and could be heard for miles; and the horrid and blasphemous threats and curses which were poured upon us in torrents, were enough to appal the stoutest heart. In the evening we had to lie down on the cold ground surrounded by a strong guard, who were only kept back by the power of God from depriving us of life. We petitioned the officers to know why we were thus treated, but they utterly refused to give us any answer, or to converse with us.[16]

For Doniphan, it had all happened too fast. The call to arms, an extermination order against upright US citizens, the betrayal and abuse of Latter-day Saint leaders, and Southern gentlemen casting aside civility for hatred. It was not right. It was a minority cause like no other he had seen. Innocent men and women about to be slaughtered by his own people—Southerners he had followed to the battlefield. Doniphan was not one to retreat, but the odds were not in his favor.

16   History, 1838–1856, volume B-1 [1 September 1834–2 November 1838], 848, josephsmithpapers.org.

CHAPTER FIVE
Defense of the Latter-day Saints

ON THE EVENING OF NOVEMBER 1, 1838, as prisoner Lyman Wight sat on the ground wondering if any good was coming from the court martial, a lieutenant approached him and said, "We do not wish to hurt you nor kill you, neither shall you be, by G—, but we have one thing against you, and that is, you are too friendly to Joe Smith, and we believe him to be a G—d—rascal." Wight replied to the lieutenant, "You may thank Joe Smith that you are not in hell this night; for had it not been for him, I would have put you there."[1]

At the court martial held outside of Far West, General Samuel Lucas presided. Austin A. King, judge of the Fifth Judicial Court Circuit, was in attendance and so was Thomas C. Birch—a district attorney—fourteen officers, and twenty preachers. More important than them all was the attendance of Brigadier General Doniphan, for he refused to sit as an idle witness like others.

In a shrill voice, familiar to most in attendance, Doniphan decried the court martial as illegal, for the prisoners had never belonged to any lawful military organization and could not have violated military law. In spite of his plausible arguments and famed theatrics that had moved previous juries and spectators

---

1 History, 1838–1856, volume D-1 [1 August 1842–1 July 1843], 1635–1636, josephsmithpapers.org.

to tears, there were no tears, or justice, at the court martial. The prisoners were found guilty of treason and condemned to death. Brigadier General Doniphan was ordered to carry out their execution:

> Sir:—You will take Joseph Smith and the other prisoners into the public square of Far West, and shoot them at 9 o'clock to-morrow morning.
> Samuel D. Lucas
> Major-General Commanding[2]

Why would General Lucas turn to Doniphan and his militia to carry out the sentence of execution, when he could have easily turned to a military leader who was not as bullheaded or willful as Doniphan? It is possible that General Lucas was angry that Doniphan had defended the Mormon prisoners and pointed out the illegalities of the court martial. No matter the answer, General Lucas was the superior officer. Obedience to his order was not only expected, it was demanded.

In willful insubordination, Doniphan replied to General Lucas,

> It is cold-blooded murder. I will not obey your order. My brigade shall march for Liberty tomorrow morning, at 8 o'clock; and if you execute these men, I will hold you responsible before an earthly tribunal, so help me God.
> A. W. Doniphan
> Brigadier-General[3]

In private, Doniphan also said to General Lucas, "You hurt one of these men if you dare and I will hold you personally

---

2 Smith, *History of the Church*, 3:246.
3 Smith, *History of the Church*, 3:246.

responsible for it, and at some other time you and I will meet again when in mortal combat and we will see who is the better man."[4]

Doniphan's refusal to comply with the order of a superior officer was a slap in the face to military rank and order. Doniphan would not have countenanced such insubordination from a junior officer in the Clay County Militia, yet, with raw courage and no regret, he defied General Lucas.

Doniphan Departs for Liberty

On the morning of November 2, 1838, Doniphan began making preparations to depart with his troops for Clay County. Hyrum Smith recalled that before Doniphan left, he

> came to us where we were under guard, to shake hands with us and bid us farewell. His first salutation was, "By God you have been sentenced by the court martial to be shot this morning; but I will be damned if I will have any of the honor of it, or any of the disgrace of it; therefore I have ordered my brigade to take up the line of march and to leave the Camp, for I consider it to be cold blooded murder, and I bid you farewell."[5]

To prisoner Lyman Wight, Doniphan said, "'Wight, your case is a d—— hard one; you are all sentenced to be shot to-morrow morning at eight o'clock on the public square in Far West. . . . I wash my hands against such cool-blooded and heartless murder.' . . . [He] also said he should move his troops, numbering three hundred, before sunrise the next morning and would not suffer them to witness such hard-hearted, cruel,

---

4 J. Wickliffe Rigdon, "I Never Knew a Time When I Did Not Know Joseph Smith," 36, quoted in Launius, *Alexander William Doniphan*, 64.
5 History, 1838–1856, volume D-1 [1 August 1842–1 July 1843], 1611, josephsmithpapers.org.

and base murder. He then shook hands with me and bade me farewell."[6]

Doniphan abandoned the prisoners and the directive to carry out the governor's extermination order when he instructed his men to leave the military encampment outside of Far West. They marched through Far West on the way to Liberty, where they were mustered out on November 5, 1838. For his eleven days of active duty and the duty of his slave in what was called the Mormon War, Doniphan received $67.35.

As for his insubordination, Doniphan was never called to account for his refusal to follow General Lucas's orders, his leaving the military encampment, or his unwillingness to execute the extermination order. When the Mormon War ended, General Lucas tried to convince Governor Lilburn W. Boggs to remove Doniphan's military commission on the basis that he disobeyed a superior officer. Governor Boggs refused to consider his request.

The Richmond Hearing

General Samuel Lucas, no doubt fearful of Doniphan's threats and wondering, if not knowing, about the illegalities of the court martial, did not insist that the prisoners be shot at the public square in Far West. Instead, he sent the prisoners to Independence, and from there, they were transported to Richmond.

On November 10, 1838, the prisoners arrived in Richmond under the guard of a well-armed militia. Two days after their arrival, on November 12, a hearing was held. Judge Austin A. King presided—the same judge who sat in the audience and listened to the court martial only a few days before. William T. Wood and Thomas C. Birch were the prosecuting attorneys. Alexander Doniphan and Amos Rees represented the prisoners. Of his defense attorneys, Joseph Smith wrote, "We could get

---

6 *Journal of History* (Board of Publication of the Reorganized Church of Jesus Christ of Latter Day Saints: 1916), 9:168.

no others in time for the trial. They are able men and will do well no doubt."[7]

A hostile crowd gathered in the circus-like atmosphere of the Richmond courthouse to observe the court proceedings. Most were convinced before the hearing began that the Mormon prisoners were guilty of high crimes. Against a backdrop of a courtroom filled with unruly men, the Richmond hearing got underway. The prosecution called forty-one witnesses—twenty Missourians and twenty-one Latter-day Saints—sworn in at the point of a bayonet.

Doniphan and Rees tried, but failed, to introduce witnesses in what was becoming a charade of justice. Doniphan said, "It was a . . . shame that these defendants should be treated in this manner; that they could not be permitted to get one witness before the court, whilst all their witnesses, even forty at a time, have been taken by force of arms and thrust into 'that . . . bull pen,' in order to prevent them from giving their testimony."[8]

For fifteen weary days, the prisoners listened to a seemingly endless parade of perjured witnesses, who verified old rumors by creating new ones. By November 28, 1838, Judge King had heard enough. He sentenced five prisoners to the Richmond Jail without bail and six to Liberty Jail to be held without bail until trial. In total frustration Doniphan exclaimed, "If a cohort of angels were to come down and declare we were clear, . . . it would all be the same, for he [Judge King] had determined from the beginning to cast us into prison."[9]

Joseph had expected more from his defense attorneys than the verdict of imprisonment to await trial. He wrote, "They have done us much harm from the beginning. . . . They

7   Letter to Emma Smith, 12 November 1838, 1, josephsmithpapers.org; spelling and punctuation modernized.
8   History, 1838–1856, volume D-1 [1 August 1842–1 July 1843], 1615, josephsmithpapers.org.
9   Sidney Rigdon, *Appeal to the American People* (1840), 2nd ed., 48, josephsmithpapers.org.

are co-workers with the mob."[10] His belief was reinforced when Doniphan presented a bill for his legal fee of $5,000. The fee was extraordinary, well beyond the expected cost for the time.

Lacking requisite funds to pay his legal fees, on November 28, 1838, the day the Richmond hearing ended, Bishop Edward Partridge executed a deed between himself and his wife, Lydia Partridge, and Alexander Doniphan and Amos Rees for 1,079.86 acres in the center of Kansas City. Rees and Doniphan accepted the acreage as payment in full even though Joseph Smith advised Doniphan

> not to take that Jackson County land in pay-
> ment of the debt, God's wrath hangs over
> Jackson County. God's people have been ruth-
> lessly driven from it, and you will live to see the
> day when it will be visited by fire and sword.
> The Lord of Hosts will sweep it with the besom
> of destruction. The fields and farms and houses
> will be destroyed, and only the chimneys will
> be left to mark the desolation.[11]

Not believing in Joseph Smith's prophetic calling, Doniphan took the property.

Liberty Jail

Of their journey to Liberty Jail, Hyrum Smith said, "We were exhibited to the inhabitants, and this course was adopted all the way, thus making a public exhibition of us, until we arrived at Liberty."[12] On December 1, 1838, the prisoners entered Liberty Jail. Making sense of what happened on a given day in the jail is near impossible, for none of the prisoners kept a daily

---

10   History, 1838–1856, volume C-1 [2 November 1838–31 July 1842], 902, josephsmithpapers.org.

11   B. H. Roberts, *History of The Church of Jesus Christ of Latter-day Saints* (Salt Lake City: Deseret News, 1905), 3:lxviii.

12   History, 1838–1856, volume D-1 [1 August 1842–1 July 1843], 1615, josephsmithpapers. org.

record. Rather, we assume that time hung heavy and there was little relief from the monotony of close confinement. There is enough scattered but cursory information to give structure to the prison experience. For example, Joseph wrote, "[Sidney] Rigdon and myself commenced this day the study of Law, under the instruction of Generals Atchison and Doniphan— They think by diligent application we can be admitted to the bar in twelve months."[13] Another example is the frequency of Doniphan's visits to the jail:

> December 21—Attorney Doniphan and Attorney Burnett.
> January 5—Attorney Burnett and Judge Joel Turnham.
> January 8—Attorney Doniphan and Attorney Burnett. [14]

The visits give evidence that Doniphan and other attorneys were actively pursuing lawful channels to assist the prisoners. On January 25, 1839, Doniphan filed a writ of habeas corpus to force the circuit court to convene. When the court came together, Judge Joel Turnham presided. After Doniphan and Peter Burnett presented their case, Sidney Rigdon asked Doniphan "to inquire of the Judge if he might speak in his own behalf." The judge replied, "Certainly." Of Rigdon's remarks, Doniphan said, "Such a burst of eloquence it was never my fortune to listen to." When Rigdon finished, spectators in the courtroom were in tears. Judge Turnham was so moved, he said, "The prisoner is discharged [from] the custody of the Court. Mr. Rigdon is free to go his way."[15]

Sidney Rigdon was released on February 5, 1839, after sixty-seven days of captivity in Liberty Jail. The five other

13 History, 1838–1856, volume B-1 [1 September 1834–2 November 1838], 819, josephsmithpapers.org.
14 *The Joseph Smith Papers*, December 21, 1838; January 5, 1839; and January 8, 1839.
15 *The Saints' Herald* 31, no. 31 (August 1884).

prisoners were remanded back to jail without bail in spite
of Doniphan's efforts. Doniphan petitioned for a change of
venue, asserting that the Latter-day Saint leaders could not get
a fair trial in this region of the state. When the change of venue
was granted, the prisoners were taken out of Liberty Jail. In
the process of moving the prisoners, they escaped. Whether
their escape was a conspiracy hatched up by state officials or
the sheriff and his deputies assigned to transport the prisoners
is conjecture. Either way, the Latter-day Saint leaders were free.

A Folk Hero

Ill will did not follow Doniphan for his defense of Latter-day
Saint leaders. He believed himself fortunate and said, "Fortune
does not shower her favors on us very often and a man should not
turn his plate bottom upwards when it does happen, but should
turn the right side up and catch all he can."[16]

Knowing that he was still popular among his constituents,
Doniphan again threw his hat into the political arena. Although
he had been approached about running for the US Congress, his
interest didn't lie in Washington—Missouri was his passion. He
accepted the Whig nomination to represent Clay County in the
Missouri House of Representatives for a second term and was
elected in 1840 by a margin of 104 votes.

While waiting for the legislative session to begin in 1840,
Doniphan had much on his mind. His wife, Jane, gave birth to
a second son, Alexander Doniphan Jr., on September 10, 1840.
With a baby and a toddler in his home, Doniphan wanted to spend
time with his little ones. Then there was also his ever-growing law
practice to consider.

As November 1840 approached, Doniphan was ready to
represent Clay County in the legislature and make a difference for
his constituents, but his heart was elsewhere. While he completed
his legislative term and tried to make a difference, not much came

16 Walter Barlow Stevens, *Centennial History of Missouri (The Center State):One Hundred
Years in the Union 1820–1921* (Chicago: S. J. Clarke Publishing Company, 1921), 2:185.

of his efforts. When his term was over, he wanted out of politics. He resumed his law practice but could not muster the same passion he had previously had. What had captured his fancy was property and investments. Doniphan was extremely successful in these new ventures. He entered into land partnerships from Clay County to the Platte River. He invested in the Liberty Insurance Company and the Hamilton Ferry on the Platte River. To say each of his investments doubled in value would not be far from the truth.

Doniphan Defends Orrin Porter Rockwell

Doniphan had not expected that his law practice would again bring him into the spotlight. After all, he was now simply part of the landed gentry and looking for his next investment. However, Doniphan's skill in the courtroom would again be needed in an unlawful case against Orrin Porter Rockwell.

On May 6, 1842, former Governor Lilburn W. Boggs was sitting in his study in Independence, when "without warning someone discharged seventeen small balls through the window into the back of the chair [in which Boggs was sitting]. Four slugs entered his neck and head; two penetrated his skull, one passed through the hollow of his neck and into his mouth, and the last embedded itself into Boggs' neck muscle."[17] Though severely injured, Boggs did not die as a result of the assassination attempt.

On circumstantial evidence, Sheriff J. H. Reynolds of Independence issued a reward of $3,000 for the capture of Orrin Porter Rockwell. On March 4, 1843, Rockwell was arrested in St. Louis. He was placed in irons and transported across the state to Independence. For nine months, Rockwell was confined in the Independence Jail. Twice he was escorted from jail to Liberty to stand trial. At the first trial, before Judge John F. Ryland on August 3, 1843, Rockwell reported,

---

17   Launius, *Alexander William Doniphan*, 79.

I was taken into Court and was asked by the Judge if I had any Council. I told him I had not, he asked if I had any means to employ a council, I answered that I had none with me that I could control.

He then said, here are a number of Counselors, if I was acquainted with any of them, I could take my choice, I told him I would make choice of Mr. Doniphan, who arose and made a speech, saying he was crowded with business, but that here are plenty of young Lawyers who could plead for me as well as he could; the Judge heard his plea and then told me he did not consider that a sufficient excuse and I could consider Mr. Doniphan my Counsel.[18]

Judge Ryland ordered Rockwell taken back to the Independence Jail so Doniphan could have time to prepare his defense.

Doniphan asked for a change of venue because animosity in Independence against Latter-day Saints still ran high. Judge Ryland agreed and ordered the Rockwell case transferred to Clay County.

In front of his former constituents and long-time friends, on December 11, 1843, Doniphan again represented a Latter-day Saint—this time defending Rockwell, a man accused of attempting to murder a former governor. That day in the courtroom in Liberty, Doniphan was at his best. He convinced Judge Austin King that Rockwell should serve a five-minute sentence for a failed jailbreak and no time for the assassination attempt he was accused of. When Judge King agreed, the courtroom erupted in praise for Doniphan, for he was truly at the top of his game—he had no equal. Whatever the spectators may have thought of Rockwell was secondary. Doniphan was the man of the hour—he had proven himself the best defense attorney in the state.

---

18   History, 1838–1856, volume E-1 [1 July 1843–30 April 1844], 1829, josephsmithpapers. org.

CHAPTER SIX
Mexican-American War

IN THE 1840S, *MANIFEST DESTINY* captured the imagination of the American people and their leaders. With the patriotic slogan *Manifest Destiny* liberally splashed across newspaper headlines, US president James K. Polk viewed his election in 1844 as a mandate to extend the nation to the Pacific Ocean. Sending a diplomatic team to negotiate the acquisition of New Mexico and California was his first step to reach the Pacific. Polk armed his negotiators with the presidential promise to assume $4.5 million in property damage due to American nationals for losses suffered in recent Mexican civil wars. This, plus his assurance of federal funds of five million dollars for New Mexico and twenty-five million dollars for California, led the negotiators to assume the offer would be accepted.

Although Polk's offer was on the side of generosity, or at least he thought so, all diplomatic posturing was rebuffed. Angered at the impasse, on January 13, 1846, President Polk ordered General Zachary Taylor to move US troops across the Nueces River and take a defensive stance on the eastern bank of the Rio Grande. Four months later, on April 24, 1846, Mexican General Mariano Arista ordered his troops to cross the Rio Grande and attack the US forces. The next day, General Arista's troops ambushed sixty-three American dragoons, killing eleven, wounding others, and capturing the rest.

General Taylor notified President Polk of the hostilities. Polk labeled the ambush an act of war and within days, Congress concurred. On May 13, 1846, the US Congress authorized President James K. Polk to enlist fifty thousand volunteers from the Ohio Valley.

Within days, Doniphan, then a thirty-eight-year-old brigadier general in the Clay County Militia, was handed a letter from Missouri Governor John C. Edwards. In the letter, Governor Edwards requested that Doniphan gather two companies of volunteers (120 men) to fight in the war against Mexico. Having a strong belief in America's Manifest Destiny, Doniphan was pleased with the assignment. He not only gathered volunteers but also made plans to enter the fight himself. As he prepared to leave his family and fortune to answer the patriotic call, he paused long enough to give power of attorney to his father-in-law, John Thornton, "to sell all my personal property & slaves and also to sell & dispose of all & any lands I own in Clay, Lafayette, Jackson, Ray, Anderson, and all other places—and to make deeds in any named therefrom to which deeds my wife will assent" in case of Doniphan's death in the Mexican-American War.[1]

Doniphan and the Missouri Volunteers at Fort Leavenworth

On June 4, 1846, Doniphan and the other Missouri volunteers departed from Liberty and were bound for Fort Leavenworth. Two days later, they arrived at the fort and were officially enlisted. Doniphan enlisted as a private. On June 7, 1846, General Kearny swore in privates and officers in Company C, First Missouri Mounted Volunteer Regiment of the Army of the West.

The majority of the volunteers were a rowdy bunch of farm boys who would not be governed by authority—especially military authority. They brought their own weapons and horses,

1 Alexander W. Doniphan, Power of Attorney, June 20, 1846, quoted in Launius, *Alexander William Doniphan*, 92.

not willing to trust government-issued anything. When ordered to
wear uniforms, they rarely complied, believing they had enlisted
in the military to fight, not to dress up. Even Doniphan wore his
own clothing, including a broad-rimmed white hat rather than a
government-issued uniform. Army officers trained at West Point
complained of the Missourians, saying the men, "unwashed and
unshaven, were ragged and dirty." To the West Point officers, the
Missourians were "listless and sickly-looking, or were sitting in
groups playing at cards, and swearing and cursing, even at the
officers."[2]

In an election of regiment officers, held on June 18, 1846,
Doniphan ran for the rank of colonel against a West Point
graduate. He won by a majority of five hundred votes, which
suggests the Missouri volunteers wanted a citizen-soldier to
lead them in battle, not a West Point officer in a fancy uniform.
It also shows the value of Doniphan's backers, who gave away
liquor for votes.

Doniphan was briefed on his duties by General Kearny.
The promotion from private to colonel was no small leap,
and General Kearny was concerned that Doniphan would be
unable to fulfill the duties required of him in his new role.
Doniphan's mission was to lead the Missouri Volunteer Militia
in battle, protect Texas, control more Mexican lands, and
broaden the boundaries of the nation to California. Doniphan
was confident he and his men could meet expectations. General
Kearny was not.

> The Genl said your men can never be soldiers, you
> indulge them too much & they will be utterly de-
> moralised and unreliable unless you adopt more
> strict and soldier like discipline. I replied Genl,
> we are 600 miles from any enemy—I fear a more
> strict discipline would break down the men &

2 George Frederick Augustus Ruxton, *Adventures in Mexico and the Rocky Mountains*
(New York: Harper & Brothers, 1848), 178.

horses—when the time comes for efficient action, you will find these men unflinching. He replied rather testily "well you will be held responsible for their efficiency." I said certainly, I would not have accepted the command of men for whom I would not be responsible in any emergency.[3]

To Santa Fe and Beyond

Doniphan and his volunteers began their long march through disputed American Indian Territory to capture the town of Santa Fe, with departures of regiment companies staggered so as not to overtax the waterways and the grass for livestock. In August 1846, when they reached Santa Fe, they learned that the Mexican government had surrendered and the regiment was to wait until General Sterling Price arrived with the second regiment of Missouri Mounted Volunteers. As Doniphan and his men waited, most found diversion in all things Spanish.

For Doniphan, he spent his time writing a code of laws for the newly incorporated territory of New Mexico. Writing the code took about a month. It comprised 115 double-columned pages—one column written in English and the other in Spanish. The code was presented to General Kearny for approval on September 21, 1846. The general sanctioned the code with limited revisions. Doniphan later said of his work, "It is astonishing, considering the short time we had been there and our limited means of information, that we should have written a code that Congress after the annexation of the territory, re-enacted and which, after thirty-five years I found still in vogue in 1881."[4]

Doniphan's love of theatrics could not be kept at bay when he learned that the Mormon Battalion was marching toward Santa Fe. When the battalion arrived, he ordered a 100-gun salute

3   Doniphan to D. C. Allen, September 20, 1883, quoted in Launius, *Alexander William Doniphan*, 96–97.
4   Allen Jones, "Alexander W. Doniphan: 'American Xenophon,'" quoted in Alexander Doniphan Committee, *The Will of Missouri*, 98.

to welcome them. No doubt he was impressed by the battalion members' patriotism in spite of the wrongs they had suffered in the nation. Doniphan walked among the soldiers of the battalion and was "pleased to find a number of old acquaintances and friends."[5]

Receiving word that he and his volunteers could leave Santa Fe and join the fighting, Doniphan looked forward to his first battle in the struggle for Manifest Destiny. However, there was a side note to attend to before confronting the Mexican armies. Doniphan received orders to reach a peace settlement with the Navajo Nation—a nation that had been at war with Mexico for years.

To fulfill his orders, he met with fourteen Navajo chiefs to discuss past problems and to assure the chiefs that better days were ahead. The chiefs agreed and signed the Treaty of Ojo del Oso. The treaty promised peace between the Navajos, neighboring tribes, and their overseers—the Army of the West.

When the peace council concluded on November 23, 1846, Doniphan was confident that peace would prevail, although there was little lasting value that came from the treaty. Hostilities between the Navajos and settlers in New Mexico raged on. It would take another generation and more sophisticated military campaigns before the Navajos were pacified.

But believing himself a fine negotiator and that he had spearheaded a lasting peace treaty, late in the year of 1846, Doniphan and his men marched to El Paso del Norte and on Christmas Day set up camp near El Braxito (outside modern-day El Paso). There, they fought in their first battle. About 50 Mexicans were killed and about 150 wounded. Doniphan didn't lose a man, although seven men were wounded. After the battle, the Missouri volunteers marched on to El Paso and then to Chihuahua City.

As Doniphan and his men neared Chihuahua, they encountered a sizable Mexican force near the Sacramento River. Although outnumbered, the volunteers defeated the Mexicans

5 Daniel Tyler, *A Concise History of the Mormon Battalion in the Mexican War 1846–1847* (Waynesboro, VA: M&R Books, 1881), 165.

and occupied Chihuahua, a city of about twenty-five hundred inhabitants. Doniphan sent a "Proclamation by the Commander in chief of the North American forces in Chihuahua" to the conquered inhabitants:

> He has taken military possession of this capitol, and has the satisfaction to assure them that complete tranquility exits therein. He invites all the citizens to return to their houses, and continue their ordinary occupations. . . . He invites the citizens of all the towns and *ranchora* to continue their traffic. . . . Lastly, we assure all good citizens, that we carry on war against the armies alone, and not against individual citizen who are unarmed.
>
> Signed, Alexander W. Doniphan,
> Commander-in-chief [6]

In late April of 1847, Doniphan and his men marched from Chihuahua City to Saltillo and joined forces with Zachary Taylor at Buena Vista. From this point on, Doniphan and his volunteers did not participate in another battle.

Although the number of battles that Doniphan and his men fought in were few, their victorious conquests put Doniphan in the same category as General Zachary Taylor and John C. Fremont. He was spoken of as an American hero—a military commander of the highest caliber. It was said of Doniphan that he paved the way for New Mexico and Arizona to be annexed in the United States.

After the Mexican-American War

After the war, Doniphan and his Missouri volunteers voyaged on the steamer *Republic* to New Orleans via the Gulf of Mexico.

---

6 "Proclamation by the Commander in-chief of the North American forces in Chihuahua," quoted in David W. Jackson, "Colonel Alexander William Doniphan: Trials on the Missouri Frontier," in Alexander Doniphan Committee, *The Will of Missouri*, 37.

News of their impending arrival reached New Orleans days before the steamer dropped anchor in port. The celebrations were riotous as the men stepped off the steamer, for all had heard of Doniphan and his conquests. After the celebrations, the Missouri volunteers received their discharge papers. They then lined up at the paymaster's office to receive back pay and allowances, which amounted to more than three hundred dollars per soldier.

From June 28 to 30, 1847, Doniphan and his men voyaged aboard the steamer *Old Hickory* up the Mississippi River to St. Louis. On July 2, 1847, the Missouri Volunteer Militia paraded through the streets of St. Louis to the "Col. Doniphan Grand March." Observing the celebration, Elizabeth Sargent penned, "The volunteers were welcomed back from Mexico, Col. Doniphan's regiment, the poor fellows looked bright and happy though sunburnt and weary. . . . The bells ringing and all looking happy and greeting them on their return from the scene of their peril and privation."[7]

Doniphan spoke to the large crowd gathered to honor him and his men. He said to his men, "You have endured much toil and hardship. It is now about to terminate. You have arrived once more in the land of civilized society."[8]

As the festivities in St. Louis were winding down, communities in northern Missouri were ready to welcome Doniphan and the volunteers. In Independence, ladies presented him with a laurel wreath, symbolic of his victories. In Gallatin, a parade was held around the town square. In his hometown of Liberty, the *Liberty Weekly Tribune* reported—

> Our community are anxiously looking for the
> Hero of Sacramento and his brave little army,
> and are prepared to give them a welcome as will

7   Elizabeth Gowen Sargent to Mother, July 10, 1847, quoted in Launius, *Alexander William Doniphan*, 193.
8   William B. McGroarty, "William H. Richardson's Journal of Doniphan's Expedition," *Missouri Historical Review* 22 no.2 (January 1928), 542.

convince them that, however much we may be divided upon some subjects, there is but one sentiment as to the manner in which they have discharged their duty.

The glorious 4th of July is close at hand and we should be most happy to hear the shrill sound of Col. Doniphan's eloquent voice on that day. We are pleased to see the spirit manifested by our citizens in making arrangements for the Dinner.[9]

For a year, Doniphan accepted invitations to celebrate his military victories. Even before the year ended, he tired of the public adulation. One of his last speeches was given in front of the volunteers: "My old fellow-soldiers, we will never all meet again. The green sod grows above many of our loved and honored comrades, and we, too, must soon obey the last call to duty. . . . That we may all be prepared for this last solemn call and the enjoyment of a glorious hereafter is the sincere prayer of your old comrade."[10]

As the celebrations wrapped up, a few of Doniphan's close associates wrote to US president James K. Polk, suggesting that Doniphan would be the ideal commander in the next US military campaign. "Hannibal-like, [he] can overcome obstacles, which to the . . . [Regular officer] are utterly unfathomable."[11] There was also talk of Doniphan becoming a candidate for governor and US senator.

Doniphan wasn't interested in these opportunities or others and politely declined. He was content to be with his wife, Jane, and his two sons, John and William.

9 *Liberty Weekly Tribune*, June 26, 1847, quoted in Launius, *Alexander William Doniphan*, 193.

10 *Address by Col. Alexander W. Doniphan: Delivered in Liberty, MO, June 5, 1872* (Liberty, MO: Advance Book and Job Printing House, 1888), 21.

11 Abiel Leonard et al., to James K. Polk, October 23, 1847, quoted in Dawson, *Doniphan's Epic March*, 200; brackets in original.

His law practice was all but gone after his yearlong absence, and he was anxious to begin anew and recapture his legal reputation. But there was the issue of his health to consider; Doniphan was plagued with lung infections. The long march across the desert and other privations of military service had taken a toll on his well-being.

Doniphan took his wife and two sons to the East to get away from having to explain again and again why he was turning down opportunities. The family visited Kentucky, Ohio, and New York, seeing relatives and friends along the way. But it was more than a family vacation. Doniphan had accepted the US presidential appointment to serve on the Board of Visitors. As a board member, he officially witnessed the examination of cadets at the US Military Academy at West Point. He spoke at their graduation ceremony on June 15, 1848, giving a stirring speech centered on important issues facing the nation:

> The world is strangely and startlingly convulsed; thrones are crumbling; dynasties are tottering to their fall; the iron heel is robbed of the power of oppression. Who can tell, in this vast whirlpool of confused elements, what results may be produced? Who can tell in its wild career, but its vortex, widening and deepening, may yet reach our own shores? . . .
>
> But one truth is clear—we cannot hide it from ourselves. God has decreed that man shall be free—"the right divine" has heard its final knell. But whether this glorious consummation is to be attained by the slow and peaceful progression of learning, of civilization and of Christianity, or the dread ordeal of war and violence, He has wisely concealed from man's feeble vision.[12]

12   A. W. Doniphan, Graduation address, delivered in the Chapel at West Point, June 15, 1848, quoted in Launius, *Alexander William Doniphan*, 207.

Throughout his speech, Doniphan paused to cough. After the speech, he quickly excused himself. The cough turned into a sore throat, followed by hoarseness and bronchitis.

Forty-year-old Doniphan was grateful to return to Liberty and watch younger men take his place. But in reality, no one took the place of the American hero of Missouri. Doniphan was still in demand, but he was content to be with his wife and his sons.

CHAPTER SEVEN
A Reversal of Fortune

WHEN DONIPHAN RETURNED FROM THE East, he was determined to rebuild his legal practice in spite of a worsening lung infection. Criminals literally lined up at his office with money in hand, hoping to hire him as their defense attorney. He took their money but was not the same theatrical orator in the courtroom. Constant coughing and hoarseness prohibited him from making long and moving speeches. He was no longer what D. C. Allen had described—"eloquent beyond description, and without doubt entitled to be classed among the greatest orators that ever lived."[1] Doniphan was unable to move juries or spectators. Judges often ruled against his clients.

Unable to heal from his lung infection, Doniphan was on the lookout for a young law partner who could be his voice in legal summations. His nephew, John Doniphan, a native of Kentucky who had studied law in Maysville, joined him in his practice. The practice began to boom again. Doniphan and his nephew were not only amicable law partners, they also became investment partners. They purchased properties all over northern Missouri and invested in railroads and banking ventures. Their most interesting

---

1   D. C. Allen, "Colonel Alexander W. Doniphan, His Life and Character," in *Doniphan's Expedition and the Conquest of New Mexico and California* (Kansas City, MO: Bryant & Douglas Book and Stationery Co., 1907), 18.

investment was the Liberty Insurance Company, a company that insured steamboats on the Missouri River. They brought together thirty investors and a capital of $50,000. Doniphan was named president of the company.

By 1853, with the youthful vigor of his nephew and his own willingness to invest in risky propositions, Doniphan had recouped his financial standing in Clay County. The next year, without campaigning or even giving one stump speech, he was elected to a third term in the state legislature. By 1860, according to the US federal census, Doniphan was worth $40,000 in real estate wealth and $6,000 in personal wealth.[2] This meant he was, at the time, one of the richest men in the state of Missouri, worth approximately 1.5 million dollars in today's currency.

Philanthropic Contributions

Being in a position to financially give back to his community, Doniphan stepped up and contributed to the educational institutions in Liberty. He served as the first Clay County superintendent (commissioner) of schools and organized the first teachers' institute.

His most long-lasting educational contribution was the establishment of the William Jewell College. At the Missouri Baptist Convention held in Boonville, Missouri, it was proposed and agreed upon that a Baptist college be established in the state of Missouri. The question was where. Boonesville, Fayette, Columbia, and Liberty were proposed as suitable college sites. Columbia had the best chance of being selected. Dr. William Jewell of Columbia offered $10,000 in land if the convention voted in favor of his hometown.

Although not a Baptist, Doniphan attended the convention and was more vocal than perhaps advisable due to his health concerns. Nevertheless, he joined with prominent Baptists in Clay to speak on behalf of a Baptist college in Liberty. Some claimed it

2   "United States Census, 1860," database with images, *FamilySearch* (https://familysearch. org/ark:/61903/1:1:MH8S-V9F : 18 February 2021), A W Doniphan, 1860.

was Doniphan's eloquence on that occasion that "won the college for his town."[3] Most claimed it was his reputation as a hero in the Mexican-American War. Whatever the reason, Liberty was selected as the college site.

Doniphan perceived that Dr. William Jewell was deeply disappointed by the decision. Though not altogether altruistic, Doniphan proposed the college be named in honor of William Jewell. When an agreement was reached, Dr. Jewell was pleased, as was Doniphan, who knew the doctor would give large donations to the college. Doniphan served periodically on the college's board of trustees.

Death of His Sons

Neither financial status nor the philanthropic turn in Doniphan's life compensated for his personal loss. He wrote,

> I was once blessed with a lovely wife and two promising boys. . . . I may say without vanity that they were the most highly educated, the most finished educations, of any boys of that age in the state; besides the ordinary classical and scientific collegiate training, each could speak and write French, Spanish, German and Italian . . . both died by painful accidents; it renders me too sad to think or write any particulars. I had provided them with private teachers from childhood and never tasked them heavily, [or] required them to plough and to hoe when I feared study was enervating them.[4]

On May 9, 1853, at age fourteen, John Thornton Doniphan died of accidental poisoning after lingering for nearly a week in pain. His obituary stated,

3   Floyd Calvin Shoemaker, "Alexander W. Doniphan, 1808–1887 Soldier, Lawyer, and Orator," in Alexander Doniphan Committee, *The Will of Missouri*, 23.
4   William B. McGroarty, "William H. Richardson's Journal of Doniphan's Expedition," *Missouri Historical Review* 22 no. 2 (January 1928), 200.

On the night of the 3d inst., feeling somewhat indisposed, he awoke an affectionate Aunt who lay adjoining, who arose and, going to her drawer, took from it, as she supposed, a dose of Salts, which she had previously prepared for herself, but which proved to be, alas! *corrosive sublimate* [mercury chloride] which had been placed in the drawer for safe keeping, as is supposed by a servant, but unfortunately without her knowledge.—This deadly poison, thus innocently given, was at once swallowed, when the fatal accident soon became evident. The most skillful medical aid was immediately called in, and the most assiduous attention rendered, but all to no effect. Stealthily thus death had made his approach, and no skill could heal the wound which he had caused the hand of kindness to inflict.[5]

John Thornton Doniphan was buried in the family plot in the Fairview Cemetery at Liberty. At his burial, his mother, Jane, had a stroke. When she had partially recovered, Doniphan took her and their son Alexander to Virginia. Doniphan wanted Jane to soak in the White Sulphur Springs in Virginia. He hoped the natural spring water would help her completely recover from the effects of the stroke. Doniphan and his family returned to Liberty in October 1853 with Jane none the better.

Five years later, as the seventeen-year-old Alexander was attending Bethany College in Virginia (now West Virginia), he drowned while swimming in a flowing river. His death occurred on May 11, 1858. His roommate James R. Rogers said of the tragic event:

---

5 *The Liberty Tribune*, "Obituary," May 13, 1853, quoted in Alexander Doniphan Committee, *The Will of Missouri*, 42.

We were foolish enough to brave the swollen
waters of a stream near by, for a bath, a perfect
mill-race. . . . [Alexander Doniphan Jr.] on the
eve of leaping into the stream, used the familiar quotation, "Darest thou, Cassius, leap with
me into this raging flood and swim to yonder
point?" In the full current of the stream, a
distance away, an exclamation of some words
escaped him, which I failed to catch. . . . His re-
mains were recovered a month later in the Ohio,
nineteen miles away. When recovered, one foot
was gone, and only by means of the other could
I alone identify the body.[6]

Doniphan received word of his son's accidental death by
telegram. The telegram was received nearly five years to the day
that he learned his firstborn son had been poisoned. Alexander
William Doniphan Jr. was buried next to his brother in the
family plot in the Fairview Cemetery at Liberty.

Although not particularly religious before the death of his
sons, Doniphan and his wife, Jane, became active members of
the Liberty Christian Church in October 1858. They formally
joined the Liberty Christian Church in November 1860. As to
Doniphan's faith in the Lord Jesus Christ, he wrote, "But for
my unchanging and undoubting faith, I should be the most
miserable of men, but I have a most implicit confidence of
again meeting my loved and lost ones in a brighter world."[7]

---

6 James R. Rogers to William E. Connelley, March 27, 1907, quoted in Connelley,
Doniphan's Expedition and the Conquest of New Mexico and California, vii–viii.
7 Settle, *Alexander William Doniphan*, 10, quoted in Launius, *Alexander William
Doniphan*, 239.

CHAPTER EIGHT
The Civil War

In December 1860, word reached Liberty that South Carolina had seceded from the Union. At the time, fifty-one-year-old Doniphan was a slave owner of four males (ages twelve to twenty-six) and one female (age eighteen). His slaves were valued at $4,000. Not only was Doniphan the owner of slaves, he was also the president of the Clay County Pro-Slavery Aid Association. For those who knew him best, his personal and public persona definitely presented an image of a wealthy slave owner with a Deep South heritage.

Doniphan had been a slaveholder since childhood and did not want to forsake his Southern upbringing. He saw no reason to question whether slavery was lawful or not. After all, his father and grandfathers for nearly two hundred years before him had owned slaves. It was their way, the Southern way.

That's why it was so shocking to friends, neighbors, and constituents when Doniphan insisted on focusing his time and talents on keeping Missouri in the Union instead of siding with South Carolina. At his own expense, he printed and distributed handbills throughout northern Missouri, announcing the date and time he would be speaking on the efficacy of Missouri remaining in the United States. On the date specified, six thousand men and women gathered on the courthouse square at Liberty to listen to their favorite orator and Mexican-American War hero. Without so much as a note, Doniphan spoke for three hours on preserving the Union, insisting that he could not fight against his country or the flag he had carried across the West.

In the days and months that followed, Doniphan flatly refused to believe that the Union could not be preserved. He played the role of a mediator between extremists on both sides of the secession issue but personally struggled to find a middle ground that valued the Union and valued the slaveholders' rights to their property. Doniphan could envision the abolition of slavery but was opposed to its *sudden* end, believing an immediate end would destroy the economy of the Southern states.

His stance as a Unionist proved problematic when his old law partner and friend, David R. Atchison, publicly supported secession. Doniphan could side with Atchison, however, in strongly opposing the election of Abraham Lincoln, believing his election would lead to border warfare. He and Atchison supported John Bell of Tennessee for US president in the 1860 election, confident that Bell was the one candidate who could keep the Union from splitting and would insist on retaining the rights of the Southern gentlemen.

The election of Abraham Lincoln was devastating to Doniphan and Atchison. The election meant war unless a compromise could be reached. Although Doniphan had put his role in the Mexican-American War behind him, he now trumpeted his conquests as if they were new trophies for all to see. The reason—he wanted to be a loud voice in the issue of secession. His military exploits gave him a platform.

On January 12, 1861, Doniphan was selected as a delegate to a countywide meeting on the secession issue held at the courthouse at Liberty. Over two thousand residents attended, forcing the meeting to be held out of doors. Doniphan gave a ninety-minute speech pleading with fellow residents to vote to remain in the Union, assuring them that compromise was possible and better days were ahead.

The Washington Peace Conference

Less than a month later, on February 4, 1861, Doniphan was at the opening meeting of the Washington Peace Conference held in the Willard Hotel in Washington, D.C. He, along with delegates from twenty-one states, knew the conference was a last-ditch effort to thwart an impending civil war. Few delegates thought the conference would turn the tide, but each hoped a miracle was possible.

At the conference, Doniphan met Abraham Lincoln. "They were asked to back up to one another to see who was the tallest, and their heights were the same."[1] Doniphan wrote to his nephew, John Doniphan, his impression of Lincoln—

> [He is] a man of no intelligence, no enlargement of views [and] easily flattered into a belief that he is a King Canute and can say to the waves of revolution "no further." The consequence is, for the time being, [that he is] the arbiter of the destinies of this mighty nation [and] if rash, may at any time ruin all beyond redemption.[2]

At the convention, it was reported that Abraham Lincoln said to Doniphan, "And this is Colonel Doniphan, who made the wonderful march from Santa Fé to Monterey against both Indians and Mexicans. Now, Colonel, permit me to say you are the only man connected with any great military enterprise who ever came up . . . to my expectations."[3]

Doniphan was not impressed and did not share Lincoln's opinion.

---

1   David W. Jackson, "Colonel Alexander William Doniphan: Trials on the Missouri Frontier," in Alexander Doniphan Committee, *The Will of Missouri*, 44.
2   Alexander Doniphan to John Doniphan, February 22, 1861, in Kathleen Bird, "Pick a Side: Doniphan's Role in Missouri's Loyalty to the Union," in Alexander Doniphan Committee, *The Will of Missouri*, 125.
3   W. L. Webb, *Battles and Biographies of Missourians, or the Civil War Period in Our State* (Kansas City, MO: Hudson-Kimberly Publishing Co., 1900), 280–281.

> It is very humiliating for an American to know
> that the present and future destiny of his country
> is wholly in the hands of one man, and that such
> a man as Lincoln—a man . . . [who is] ridicu-
> lously vain and fantastic as a country boy with his
> first red morocco hat. . . . Jesting aside, old Abe is
> simply an ignorant country buffoon who makes
> about as good stump speeches as Jim Craig.[4]

At the conference, Doniphan supported a compromise that extended the Missouri line to the Pacific and allowed slavery south of the line, but the compromise went nowhere. He concluded that the delegates had no intention of reaching a compromise, as each pushed his own views—views that too often mirrored the warlike stance of Lincoln.

For a moment at the conference, Doniphan was swayed to consider Missouri joining the Southern Confederacy. He wrote, "The border slave states must stand or fall together as a unit and by one act, and form a new government or *go with the South*, and this last is best. As one respectable republic in numbers and power is better than twenty little rickety concerns."[5] But regaining his conviction of national unity, Doniphan pushed forward to find a suitable compromise that preserved the Union and the dignity of the South. But no matter his argument or his legendary status as an American hero, delegates turned a deaf ear to his reasoning. As the conference drew to a close on February 27, Doniphan still believed himself "a Union man. I go for the whole Union, the entire Union. I go for it North, South, East, and West. I do not intend to bring about a calamity that will destroy the Border Slave States and the whole Union."[6]

---

4 Alexander Doniphan to John Doniphan, February 22, 1861, in Susan Easton Black, "Alexander W. Doniphan: In Defense of Mormons," in Alexander Doniphan Committee, *The Will of Missouri*, 76.

5 Alexander Doniphan to John Doniphan, February 22, 1861, quoted in Dawson, *Doniphan's Epic March*, 215; italics in original.

6 Jackson, "Colonel Alexander William Doniphan: Trials on the Missouri Frontier," in Alexander Doniphan Committee, *The Will of Missouri*, 44.

When he returned to Missouri, Doniphan found old friends unwilling to listen to his views. They were entrenched in Southern ways and did not want to hear more about preserving the Union. Doniphan pushed his point and, in so doing, created ill will and distrust, even though he had worked to secure the rights of both sides of the sectional debate.

Amid what was soon becoming a firestorm of accusations, Doniphan received an appointment from newly elected Governor Willard Preble Hall of Missouri to work part-time as a state claims agent—tasked with assisting widows, orphans, and disabled soldiers in processing financial claims. To fulfill the appointment, Doniphan would need to live in St. Louis, a city that had room for an attorney who wanted the Union preserved.

Relieved at receiving the appointment, or at having an excuse to move away from argumentative friends, Doniphan took his wife to St. Louis and set up a law office in the downtown area. He formed a partnership with attorney William S. Field of Lafayette County, a man who had also withdrawn to St. Louis to get away from talk of secession. Field, like Doniphan, wanted unity in the nation. In the end, Missouri did not vote to secede from the Union. Doniphan was confident his voice had been heard.

Civil War

Doniphan and his partner, Field, built up their St. Louis law practice by representing businessmen with deep pockets in tobacco. Doniphan was no stranger to deep pockets or the Southern pride of his clients. He still owned lands in northern Missouri but often wondered if his lands were worthless given the volatile, warlike crisis on the western Missouri border. He had heard the town of Liberty was rife with Confederate and Union soldiers. And as for other towns along the border, ad hoc "guerilla" organizations were committing acts of terrorism on a level of violence not seen in other parts of the state.

Several of his old friends, even those who had fought alongside him in the Mexican-American War, were fighting for the Confederacy and wondering why Doniphan had not joined them. Missouri Governor Claiborne Fox Jackson offered Doniphan a commission in the Missouri State Guard, but he declined. Doniphan maintained a neutral position for the duration of the war. Although he was appalled by the brutality that flashed across headlines, he stayed on the sidelines as a non-fighting advocate for the Union.

With the fall 1864 election of Thomas Fletcher as governor of Missouri, Doniphan was notified that his services as the state claims agent were no longer needed. He left office on January 25, 1865, turning his clients over to George Hillgaertner, a confirmed abolitionist.

Difficult days followed for Doniphan and the state of Missouri. He wrote, "An *episode* in the history of our country dark & saddening, ruins every where . . . thousands of our best citizens were imprisoned and hundreds shot for that mythical & undefinable something called Southern Sympathy."[7]

Reflecting on the Aftermath of the Civil War

As for Doniphan personally, the war had a devastating effect on his financial standing and entrepreneurial drive. Property he had acquired in Jackson County for defending Joseph Smith and other Latter-day Saints was worthless. He visited that land and found farms destroyed and farmhouses burned. He told his brother-in-law Leonidas M. Lawson "that the devastation of Jackson County forcibly reminded him of the remarkable prediction of the Mormon prophet."[8] The prediction uttered by Joseph Smith in late November 1838 was that "God's wrath hangs over Jackson County. God's people have been ruthlessly driven from it, and you

---

7 Alexander W. Doniphan to D. C. Allen, November 10, 1874, quoted in Launius, *Alexander William Doniphan*, 266.
8 Junius F. Wells, "A Prophecy and its Fulfillment," *Improvement Era* 6 no. 1 (November 1902), 9.

will live to see the day when it will be visited by fire and sword."[9]
Not a believer in the prophetic calling of Joseph Smith, Doniphan
had taken the property as payment in full for his legal work.

To keep his Jackson property and other properties, Doniphan
had to take out loans, borrow cash to keep creditors off his
doorstep, mortgage some of his Clay County property, and sell
property at a greatly reduced price. Then there was the issue
of Clay County fathers—friends who had stood in crowds to
applaud him—seizing his property and selling it to pay back taxes.
Doniphan wrote to D. C. Allen on November 3, 1865,

> I have been so embarrassed with old debts that
> I often anticipate my income to pay them to
> avoid the notifications of continued duns. I
> have paid off my debts as rapidly as I could
> and my friends from Liberty & other places
> seeing my condition & constant labor were
> ashamed to present their claims in person—
> but left them with shoemakers, grocery keepers
> & gamblers to be presented as soon as they got
> out of town. I thank God thus far I have met
> them all—although I have been unable to col-
> lect one Dollar of all my old debts, or sell one
> acre of land.[10]

9   Roberts, *Comprehensive History of the Church*, 3:lxviii.
10   Alexander W. Doniphan to D. C. Allen, November 3, 1865, quoted in Launius,
Alexander William Doniphan, 272.

CHAPTER NINE
His Last Years

NEVER ABLE TO FIND A hometown feeling in St. Louis, Doniphan and Jane packed their possessions and moved back to the western border of Missouri. They did not return to Liberty, where they had lived for nearly thirty years and where they had buried their sons. They were still smarting over friends rejecting them because of Doniphan's unwavering stance on the Civil War.

In February 1868, Doniphan and Jane moved to Richmond, a small town about fifty miles east of Liberty. Doniphan purchased a home near the center of town on what is now South Camden Avenue. Although the home fit the time period, there was nothing lavish about the exterior. Inside the home was a different story. The mahogany furniture bespoke their wealth of yesteryear. Joining them in Richmond was Jane's father, John Thornton, who needed special care for a few months.

As Doniphan put down roots and started anew, he did what he had always done—opened a law practice. Joining him in his law practice was Christopher T. Garner, a distant cousin of his wife. The practice was familiar but lacked the success of days gone by. What brought Doniphan pleasure was being one of the founders of the Ray County Savings Bank located on the southeast corner of College and Main Streets in Richmond. The bank had a capital of $100,000. Doniphan served as president.

With the war over and a money stream in place, Doniphan and Jane thought it was time to make travel plans. Jane traveled by train to New York City to be with her sister. Doniphan attended a session of the Missouri Supreme Court in Jefferson City before joining her. In New York City, they enjoyed the sights and sounds of Northern culture. When Jane decided to stay with her sister longer, Doniphan returned alone by train to Richmond, not knowing that this was the last time he would see his wife.

Upon returning to Richmond, Doniphan received a telegram informing him that Jane's health was rapidly deteriorating. He quickly made arrangements to return to New York City, but before he could leave Richmond, a second telegram informed him of his wife's death on July 19, 1873. Jane died from a pulmonary hemorrhage at age fifty-one. Her obituary reads, "We are pained to learn of the death of Mrs. Jane Doniphan, wife of Gen. A. W. Doniphan of Richmond, Mo. . . . She had been a member of the Christian church for over thirty years, and her life of pure Christian charity attested a faith firmly founded."[1]

It was said that Jane's death threw a long shadow across Doniphan's path. He never married again, although he lived another fourteen years. Five years after her death, on May 6, 1878, Doniphan wrote to his cousin about Jane: "My own wife was such a gentle loving woman, yet with an intellect a man of culture might have envied; the loss is the misery of my life. I trace much of my suffering although physical to suffering the agony of the heart. In early life I might have had the wound seared over, in my energetic devotion to business."[2]

Months after her passing, Doniphan moved from his spacious home in Richmond to a boardinghouse about a block from the Ray County Savings Bank. The boardinghouse was one of the finest in the county. Proprietors William B. Huggins and his wife were kind to Doniphan, especially Mrs. Huggins, who doted on him. Her care was much appreciated, for his lung infection

1 "Death of an Excellent Lady," *The Missouri Republican*, July 25, 1873.
2 McGroarty, "William H. Richardson's Journal of Doniphan's Expedition," *Missouri Historical Review* 22 no. 2 (January 1928), 204–205.

was getting the better of him. After being bedridden for weeks, Doniphan wrote,

> I cannot live long unless I can find in some other climate a rejuvenating power to at least *patch* me up—A hotel . . . is best for me when sick—I can order what I please and pay for all extra trouble.[3]

By May 1874, Doniphan's health was better. He made plans to travel west, thinking the climate would be agreeable to his health. He traveled first class in sleeping cars and stayed in elegant hotels. He had a brief stay in the Townsend House in Salt Lake City, where he was treated with great kindness by Latter-day Saints who welcomed him as a hero, not for his conquests in the Mexican-American War but for his role in the Mormon War in Missouri. He returned to Richmond in the fall of 1875, exhilarated by his adventure and feeling slightly better.

By 1876 his old health complaint had returned. He concluded it was time to stop practicing law and wrote,

> I abandoned it [law] last year—brain work was injuring me. . . . I am now president of a little Bank, reading, travelling, and visiting some. . . . I am now an old man, sixty-seven, and after an active and not uneventful life—greatly varied with sunshine and shadow—I am now isolated and alone; like the tall oak whose graceful boughs and delicate foliage has been torn ruthlessly away by the bolt of heaven and the old trunk is left standing awaiting the sure process of decay and death . . .
>
> I am now boarding at a Hotel with no one of my family in the county. It is a great

---

3   Alexander W. Doniphan to Henry L. Routt, April 9, 1874, quoted in Launius, *Alexander William Doniphan*, 275; Alexander W. Doniphan to Sister Caroline, April 3, 1878, quoted in Launius, *Alexander William Doniphan*, 277.

change but far better than to live in the family
of another. You can make a hotel a sort of home
by using money and being quiet and concil-
iatory—and the family are old acquaintances
and very kind to me.[4]

Doniphan made at least one more trip west, taking the same
route he had walked in 1846 with the Missouri volunteers.
It was with nostalgic feelings he reported, "Civilization has
changed the physique of the country greatly, towns, villages and
cities having taken the place of the wigwam." He reflected on
his earlier journey and wrote, "I was then young, hopeful and
ambitious—my position novel and exciting—everything was
before me. . . . I had the ambition of most young men, had
children to inherit my fortunes, great and small—now Alas? I
am only seeking an asylum."[5]

After his last trip west, Doniphan was content to live out
his days in Richmond. He stepped down as bank president in
1880. He served on the board of directors of the bank, but his
position was more honorary than active. On his seventy-fifth
birthday, he wrote to his longtime friend D. C. Allen.

Looking back at a glance the time seems short—
and when I estimate the few things I have done
worth recording and remembering the time seems
even shorter. . . . I am aware that I have some
admiring friends who regard my professional life
to have been active and successful—and it would
be unpardonable—if not contemptible affecta-
tion not to agree with them. . . . The episodes
of my life, mere lucky accidents mainly[;] my
only ambition in truth was to be esteemed the
best jury lawyer & advocate in the counties where

---

4   McGroarty, *Missouri Historical Review*, 200–202.
5   Alexander W. Doniphan to Emma Doniphan, September 12, 1876, quoted in Launius,
Alexander William Doniphan, 278.

I practiced. . . . As far as moral honor and true
manhood is concerned I have no twinges of con-
science—not what I have done but what I have
failed to do, causes my regrets. It is a grand but
peaceful thought—that although the lamp of
life will soon be extinguished the work that has
been done or failed to do, will continue through
eternity.[6]

Continuing Latter-day Saint Connections

As the days passed into months, Doniphan grew weary
of spending each day in the hotel. He often walked the main
square of Richmond looking for friends to converse with.
Some claimed it took him a whole hour to walk the square for
so many admirers wanted to talk to him.

Of those he spoke with, David Whitmer was one man in
urgent need of help. Whitmer had been confronted with rumors
that he had denied his testimony of the gold plates, the angel
Moroni, and the Book of Mormon. Wanting to stop rumors,
Whitmer asked Doniphan to listen to his testimony. Doniphan
agreed. "[My] testimony as recorded in the Book of Mormon
is absolutely true, just as it is written there," Whitmer said.[7] On
March 19, 1881, he asked Doniphan to join with others in
Richmond and sign an affidavit attesting to his moral integrity.
Doniphan agreed and signed the following:

> We, the undersigned citizens of Richmond, [Ray
> County,] M[issouri] where David Whitmer, Sr
> has resided since the year AD 1838, Certify that
> we have been long and intimately acquainted
> with him, and know him to be a man of the

6   Alexander W. Doniphan to D. C. Allen, July 9, 1883, quoted in Launius, *Alexander William Doniphan*, 279; brackets in original.
7   "Mormonism," *Millennial Star* 43 (July 1881), 437.

highest integrity, and of undoubted truth and veracity.[8]

Other Latter-day Saints also sought an audience with Doniphan. On April 13, 1882, John Morgan and Matthias F. Cowley called on him at the boardinghouse. On June 29, 1884, leaders of the Reorganized Church of Jesus Christ of Latter Day Saints, Heman C. Smith and William H. Kelley, reported,

> We called on General Doniphan, who received us kindly, and expressed himself as being glad to meet us. He said the Mormons lived neighbors to him while they were in Clay County, and they were a moral people. . . . The General informed us that he had examined the original manuscript [of the Book of Mormon], and being acquainted with Oliver Cowdery's handwriting, was positive it was principally written by him.[9]

Death of Alexander Doniphan

When the US Congress passed the Mexican War Pension Act on January 29, 1887, Doniphan filed for a military pension and a bounty land claim of 160 acres. The Pension Office approved his pension and claim. Three months later, on Monday, August 8, 1887, Doniphan died of bronchitis and congestion at the Hugginses' boardinghouse at age seventy-nine. A few old friends were at his side.

At his funeral, Reverend J. A. Dearborn, a minister of the Christian Church at Liberty, presided. D. C. Allen gave the eulogy and said, "I never knew any one whose perception of right and wrong was so strong. I never knew of his doing or saying

---

8   David Whitmer, Proclamation, 19 March 1881; cited in Dan Vogel ed., *Early Mormon Documents* 5 vols. (Salt Lake City: Signature Books, 2003), 5:70.
9   *Journal of History* (Board of Publication of the Reorganized Church of Jesus Christ of Latter Day Saints: 1903), 4:449.

an unworthy thing, and never knew a better man."[10] Pallbearers were men who had fought alongside Doniphan in the Mexican-American War. His body was taken to Liberty, where he was buried in the family plot next to his wife, Jane, and his sons in the Fairview Cemetery. On his tombstone was etched, "An Orator, Jurist, Statesman, Soldier, and a Christian."[11]

In his last will and testament, Doniphan left $500 to Mrs. Huggins of the boardinghouse in "gratitude for her uniform friendship in sickness and in health."[12]

In Honorable Remembrance

Alexander Doniphan has not been forgotten with the passage of time. His name has been held in honorable remembrance for generations. Let us consider a few of these remembrances—

- In Latter-day Saint congregations throughout the world, he is spoken of as the man who courageously defied the order of a superior officer and, in so doing, saved the life of the Prophet Joseph Smith.
- Books have been written of his life and military conquests in the Mexican-American War.
- Doniphan County, Kansas, is named in his honor.
- The town of Doniphan in Ripley County, Missouri, is named in his honor.
- The Doniphan Chapter of the Daughters of the American Revolution is named in his honor.
- A large portrait of Doniphan is in the Hall of Fame at Fort Leavenworth, Kansas.
- A heroic-size statue of Doniphan is located on the courthouse square in Richmond, Missouri. The inscription on the statue reads, "On the roster of the great soldiers of the earth, must always stand in a halo

---

10   "D. C. Allen's Remarks," *The Gazette* (August 1887), quoted in Launius, *Alexander William Doniphan*, 280.

11   Fairview Cemetery (Liberty, Missouri), Alexander William Doniphan tombstone epitaph.

12   "Will of A. W. Doniphan," quoted in Launius, *Alexander William Doniphan*, 277.

of glory the name of Colonel Alexander W. Doniphan of Missouri."

- Missouri Highway 152, which runs through Clay and Platte County, Missouri, was renamed Doniphan Highway by the Missouri Department of Transportation.
- The Alexander Doniphan Elementary School in Liberty was named in his honor.
- Camp Doniphan, located next to Fort Still in Oklahoma, was named in his honor.
- The John F. Kennedy Pulitzer Prize–winning book *Profiles in Courage* (1956) was so successful that twenty-six episodes based on the book were presented on television. Episode Ten in the television series was based on the role of Doniphan in the Mormon War. Peter Lawford, a popular Hollywood actor and the brother-in-law of President John F. Kennedy, played the role of Doniphan.
- The Alexander Doniphan Heritage Society at the William Jewel College recognizes men in the graduating class who demonstrate leadership and strong academics.
- Governor Mel Carnahan proclaimed October 27, 1994, as Alexander Doniphan Day in Missouri.
- Doniphan Drive in El Paso, Texas, is named in his honor.
- A bronze bust of Doniphan is on permanent display in the Missouri State Capitol rotunda in Jefferson City.

There will be remembrances in the future as more come to know the man whose moral compass could not be swayed.

Conclusion

Alexander Doniphan was a man with admirers on every hand, but few who mirrored his actions. It was not that they didn't try; they just didn't have his Southern upbringing or his unwavering moral sense of right and wrong. Doniphan held opinions that were rarely popular with the majority, but people's disagreement didn't bother him. If there was an unpopular stance, he was willing to back it. If there was a fight to protect an underdog, he was the first to jump into the fray. None could call him a coward in the political arena, in the courtroom, or in battle.

Standing six foot four in height, Doniphan could not physically be ignored. His outward appearance alone suggested the world was his for the taking. He wasn't looking to make a big splash in the world; he was just looking to make a difference. He didn't want to be cantankerous, but he wasn't about to be pushed aside. Despite his uncompromising stances, those who knew him best admired him most. The reason for their admiration? Doniphan was a brave man with a nobleness of soul and a fierce loyalty to moral correctness.

He is extolled for his role in the Mexican-American War, his work in the Missouri legislature, and his courtroom persona. But to Latter-day Saints worldwide, Doniphan will always be the military officer who would not kill the Prophet Joseph Smith. Of this American hero, Elder George A. Smith said,

> There are few men whose names have been identified with the history of our Church, with more pleasant feelings to its members, than General Doniphan. During a long career of persecution, abuse and oppression, characters occasionally present themselves like stars of the first magnitude in defence [sic] of right, who are willing, notwithstanding the unpopularity that may attach to it, to stand up and protest against mob violence, murder, abuse, or the destruction of property and constitutional rights.[13]

Such a man was Alexander Doniphan—"An Orator, Jurist, Statesman, Soldier, and a Christian."[14]

---

13 George A. Smith, "General Doniphan's Connection With the Early History of the Church—Persecutions of the Saints—Mormon Battalion—Hardships Experienced in the Settlement of Utah—Plurality of Wives," *Journal of Discourses* 17:91.

14 Fairview Cemetery (Liberty, Missouri), Alexander William Doniphan tombstone epitaph.

CHRONOLOGY
of Alexander William Doniphan

July 9, 1808	Born the youngest son of Joseph Doniphan and Anne Fowke Smith near Maysville, Kentucky.
March 12, 1813	Death of his father; receives inheritance of farmland and a slave named Stephen.
1822–1826	Student at the Augusta Methodist Episcopal Academy in Augusta, Kentucky.
1827–1829	Is tutored in the study of law by the Honorable Martin P. Marshall in Augusta, Kentucky.
1829	Passes the bar exam in Kentucky; petitions the Ohio Supreme Court for admission to the state bar in Ohio.
April 19, 1830	Petitions the Missouri Supreme Court for admission to the state bar of Missouri.
1830	Settles in Lexington, Missouri; opens a law office on courthouse square in Lexington; becomes an attorney in the Fifth Judicial District Court.

Spring 1831	Meets missionaries called to the borders of the Lamanites; employs Peter Whitmer Jr. to make him a suit of clothes.
May 1833	Moves to Liberty, Missouri; becomes a law partner of David Rice Atchison; is appointed an officer in the Liberty Blues Militia.
Fall 1833	Defends the Latter-day Saints of Jackson County, Missouri.
December 6, 1833	Drafts a letter to Governor Daniel Dunklin asking that Latter-day Saints be restored to their lands in Jackson County and be protected by the militia.
June 16, 1836	Speaks against forcibly removing Latter-day Saints from Clay County, Missouri.
1836	Represents Clay County in the Missouri House of Representatives.
December 23, 1836	Introduces a bill to create Caldwell and Daviess Counties in the Missouri House of Representatives; Governor Lilburn W. Boggs signs the bill into law on December 29, 1836.
December 21, 1837	Marries Elizabeth Jane Thornton at the Old School Baptist Church in Liberty, Missouri.
September 18, 1838	Son, John Thornton Doniphan, is born in Liberty, Missouri.
October 25, 1838	Is commissioned a brigadier general in the Clay County Militia; mobilizes the Clay County Militia to put down a Mormon uprising.
October 30, 1838	Begins negotiations between Latter-day Saints and Missouri militias.
October 31, 1838	Witnesses the betrayal of Joseph Smith and other Latter-day Saint leaders by George Hinkle.

November 1, 1838	Attends court martial held against Latter-day Saint prisoners; is ordered to take Joseph Smith and the other Latter-day Saint prisoners to the public square in Far West and shoot them at 9:00 a.m. on November 2, 1838; defies the orders of a superior-ranking officer.
November 2, 1838	Marches with his men to Liberty, Missouri.
November 12–28, 1838	Defends Joseph Smith and fellow prisoners at the Richmond hearing; Judge Austin A. King presides.
December 1838	Joseph Smith and Sidney Rigdon study law under his tutelage.
January 25, 1839	Defends Latter-day Saint prisoners incarcerated in Liberty Jail before Judge Joel Turnham.
1840	Represents Clay County for the second term in the Missouri House of Representatives.
September 10, 1840	Birth of son, Alexander William Doniphan Jr.
1841–1842	Enters land and business partnerships from Clay County to the Platte River; invests in the Liberty Insurance Company; invests in the Hamilton Ferry on the Platte River.
December 11, 1843	Convinces Judge John F. Ryland that Orrin Porter Rockwell should serve a "five minute sentence."
May 1846	Gathers two companies of volunteers (120 men) to fight in the war against Mexico.
June 6, 1846	Enlists as a private in the Army of the West.
June 18, 1846	Is elected colonel of the Missouri Volunteer Militia in the Mexican-American War.

September 21, 1846	Writes a law code for the newly incorporated territory of New Mexico.
November–December 1846	Negotiates the Treaty of Ojo del Oso with the Navajos; fights in the Battle of El Braxito and the Battle of Sacramento River.
April 18, 1847	Marches with the Missouri Volunteer Militia from Chihuahua City to Saltillo; joins forces with Zachary Taylor at Buena Vista.
June 1847	Is discharged from the military at New Orleans, Louisiana.
June 15, 1848	Speaks at the graduation ceremony held at the US Military Academy at West Point.
May 9, 1853	Death of son John Thornton Doniphan in Liberty, Missouri.
1854	Represents Clay County for a third term in the Missouri House of Representatives.
May 11, 1858	Death of son Alexander William Doniphan Jr. in Virginia.
November 1860	Joins the Liberty Christian Church.
February 1861	Attends Washington Peace Conference held in Washington, D.C.
1861	Accepts appointment as a state claims agent; moves to St. Louis, Missouri.
1868	Moves to Richmond, Missouri; becomes president of the Ray County Savings Bank.
July 19, 1873	Death of his wife, Elizabeth Jane Doniphan, in New York City.
1873	Moves into William B. Huggins's boardinghouse in Richmond, Missouri.

1874	Journeys to the Rocky Mountains; is welcomed as a hero by Latter-day Saints in Salt Lake City.
1876–1880	Stops practicing law; resigns as president of the Ray County Savings Bank.
August 8, 1887	Dies at William B. Huggins's boardinghouse in Richmond, Missouri, at age seventy-nine.
August 1887	Is buried in the family plot at the Fairview Cemetery in Liberty, Missouri.

ABOUT THE AUTHOR

DR. SUSAN EASTON BLACK JOINED the faculty of Brigham Young University in 1978 and taught Church history and doctrine until she retired to serve missions with her husband, George Durrant. She is the past associate dean of General Education and Honors and the director of Church History in the Religious Studies Center. For her research and writing, Susan has been the recipient of numerous academic awards. She received the Karl G. Maeser Distinguished Faculty Lecturer Award in 2000, the highest award given a professor on the BYU campus. Susan has authored, edited, and compiled more than 100 books and 300 articles.